Series Editor **Mike Burghall**

# Using the Mother Tongue

## Making the most of the learner's language

Sheelagh Deller
Mario Rinvolucri

with a prologue by Luke Prodromou

Published by
First Person Publishing /
ENGLISH TEACHING *professional*
Tech West House
10 Warple Way
London W3 0UE

DELTA PUBLISHING
39 Alexandra Road
Addlestone
Surrey KT15 2PQ

First published 2002

ISBN  0 954198 61 1

Designed by Christine Cox
Cover illustration by Phillip Burrows
Project managed by Chris Hartley
Printed by The Baskerville Press Ltd

**Acknowledgements**
The authors would like to thank:

The many learners who have made it clear to us that they
need to be allowed to refer to their mother tongue.

Those people in the profession who have recently been
publicly advocating a change of attitude towards using the
mother tongue.

Tim Hahn for his contributions both on paper and in
conversation.

Mike Burghall for his enthusiasm and clarity.

Tanya Whatling for her invaluable help, sound comments
and patience.

ENGLISH TEACHING *professional* and DELTA PUBLISHING for
having the courage to publish what could be considered a
controversial book.

Each other for understanding and appreciating our
differences and similarities – a contrastive approach!

# Personal Prefaces

## Sheelagh Deller

I was once working with a group of English teachers of French. We did an activity that involved using the mother tongue as a tool to teach and practise vocabulary. The feedback was very interesting. One teacher said, 'I enjoyed it and it works. But I'll never use it. I don't agree with using the mother tongue in class. And anyway, we aren't allowed to.'

How very sad. An activity which is enjoyable **and** works, and yet this teacher wouldn't use it because for her, using the mother tongue is a no-no.

This really struck a chord with me. I've been lucky to spend most of my teaching life in situations where I can be pretty autonomous about how I teach. And, in spite of the fact that more often than not I teach multilingual classes, or students whose language I don't speak, I have often found myself encouraging them to think and communicate more bilingually.

The mother tongue taboo has been with us for a long time but fortunately now things seem to be changing. I believe that many teachers have continued to use the mother tongue because it is both necessary and effective. However, teachers may well have been using it privately and secretly – and certainly not in front of inspectors or colleagues! So we just add to the guilt feelings that we as teachers are so good at having.

The purpose of this book, therefore, is to free us of this guilt and to think about ways of using the mother tongue, not just for convenience but as a real living and vital resource for our learners. After all, it is what they bring in to our classrooms and as such it cannot be ignored. It will always be in their heads, so why can't it come out of our mouths if it can encourage and foster understanding and learning. Let's be purposeful and intelligent about using the mother tongue and acknowledge it to be the important resource it obviously is.

## Mario Rinvolucri

Thirty years ago I was so much part of the Direct Method orthodoxy of the day that I frowned on bilingual dictionaries and one day found myself miming the word 'although' in an elementary class! There were brilliant people in the class: one student whispered to another, 'He mean "but"?'

It was meeting the work of Charles Curran and using his Community Language Learning technique with beginners that made me realise that the mother tongue is the womb from which the second language is born. Curran was a theologian and a counsellor and he had no Direct Method hang-ups. For him it was obvious that beginner learners, in teenage and adulthood, would express themselves in their mother tongue and that this would then need to be translated for them into the target language before they could themselves say it in the target language.

Why did I need to wait till I came across Curran's work to free myself from the bizarre ban on mother tongue in the foreign language classroom? After all, I had lived in a mixed language situation as a child. With English as my mother tongue, I began to be exposed to Italian in the home from the age of three. I would naturally produce utterances like:

| Mi | dai | l'olio | e | vinegar? |
|----|-----|--------|---|----------|
| To me | give | the oil | and | |

The syntax and most of the words were Italian, but 'vinegar' stayed obstinately in mother tongue. The sentence was quite clear to my bilingual interlocutors.

When I learnt Spanish academically at secondary school, I wore out a couple of bilingual dictionaries in my keenness to launch from the mother tongue into the unclear waters of the target language. In my teenage foreign language work, mother tongue was the semantic bedrock that all my explorations built up from. How had I managed to exclude my real experience as a language **learner** from my practice as a language **teacher** for so many years?

This book is a kind of apology to my students in the 1970's who had to smuggle their bilingual dictionaries into my classroom and hide them under the table. It is also a salute to the traditional teaching systems in places like China and Japan where it has always been understood that mother tongue is necessary. It offers natural grammar-translation teachers the beginnings of a new, diversified and humanised methodology that respects their basic intuition, but that offers their students a more lively experience of the language classroom.

# Prologue

## The Liberating Role of the Mother Tongue

Until recently, the mother tongue in the ELT classroom has been a 'skeleton in the cupboard'. The metaphor is apt insofar as we have for a long time treated the mother tongue as a 'taboo' subject, a source of embarrassment and, on the part of non-native speaker teachers in particular, a symptom of their failure to 'teach properly'.

We need to break the stranglehold of negative perceptions of the mother tongue in the classroom. We need new, more positive metaphors for the role of the mother tongue.

The following metaphors may help put some flesh on the skeleton:

- a drug (though it has therapeutic potential, it can damage your health and may become addictive)

- a reservoir (a resource from which we draw)

- a wall (for writing on or an obstacle to progress?)

- a crutch (it can help us get by in a lesson, but it is recognition of weakness)

- a lubricant (it keeps the wheels of a lesson moving smoothly; it thus saves time).

- a window (which opens out into the world outside the classroom; if we look through it we see the students' previous learning experience, their interests, their knowledge of the world, their culture)

These metaphors suggest the potential for **using** the mother tongue, but also alert us to the danger of **abusing** the mother tongue. Our strategic objective will continue to be maximum interaction in the target language and the role of the mother tongue will be to enrich the quality and the quantity of that interaction in the classroom, not to restrict or impoverish it.

Ever since the prevalence of 'direct methods' in ELT and the ascendancy of the native speaker as the best model for good teaching practice, 'teaching properly' has meant using 'only English' and banishing the students' mother tongue from the classroom. This dominance of the native speaker teacher of English in our profession is now being questioned and with it the stigmatising of the mother tongue in foreign language education. The native speaker has been, in a practical sense, a 'monolingual teacher' whose global mobility made the knowledge and use of the students' mother tongue an unwelcome encumbrance. The results have been disastrous for the vast majority of teachers of English worldwide who happen to be non-native speakers of the language. The non-native speaker or bilingual teacher has been denied access by a misguided ELT orthodoxy to an enormously powerful tool: the students' mother tongue, and, by extension, their mother culture.

In educational terms, it is a gross contradiction to teach a language, any language (that most human of cognitive and affective faculties), without reference to and creative deployment of the students' mother tongue and, by extension, their mother culture. In first language education, it would be unthinkable to propose the exclusion of the students' linguistic culture from the classroom.

However, a skeleton in the cupboard is something most people probably have, in one form or another. The irony in ELT since 'direct methods' became the official orthodoxy is that most non-native speaker teachers of English have quietly been using the mother tongue, to a lesser or greater extent. The skeleton has been there all the time, we just haven't wanted to talk about it. The mother tongue has been used surreptitiously and haphazardly and, as a result, it may not have been used to good effect. Its potential as a resource has been cramped and distorted by the guilt and prohibitions that have accompanied its use.

**Luke Prodromou**

# Contents

# Introduction

Hans Anderson has a story in which an emperor is tricked by some tailors into solemnly walking through the capital with no clothes on. Because of his status, the townspeople persuade themselves to think he is wearing sumptuous robes. One child, however, shouts out:

MUMMY, WHY HAS THE EMPEROR GOT NO CLOTHES ON?

This book shouts out:

DON'T THE STUDENTS HAVE A MOTHER TONGUE?

Orthodox thinking over the past forty years in the US, UK and Europe has been that the use of mother tongue should be excluded from the foreign language classroom.

Our contention is, on the contrary, that **mother** tongue (MT), is indeed the mother of the second, third and fourth languages. It is from this womb that the new languages are born in the student's mind, so to exclude MT from the English classroom is like trying to wean a baby on day one of their life.

What we propose is that teachers use the students' mother tongue in clearly-defined circumstances (see Part A, Section 1) and in the carefully crafted activities that make up the main body of this book.

The overriding aim of the book is that your students should willingly come to reduce their dependence on MT. Paradoxically, this will come about earlier in their learning process than would be the case if MT were 'banned' from the classroom.

The judicious use of MT in the classroom benefits everyone.

## Benefits for the Student

Students feel safe and grounded in the English classroom.

- At beginner level in particular, students' progress is much faster.

- At the upper levels, judicious use of MT allows students to fully enjoy the exercise of their linguistic intelligence.

- English grammar can be better understood by looking into the MT grammar mirror.

- New items of English vocabulary can be introduced in a clear and defined way, with students learning where a word is the same or different in their MT.

## Benefits for the Teacher

- This book breaks the constraints imposed by the taboo of 'no mother tongue in the English classroom'. It offers varied and student-centred activities exploiting this important resource. If you have always made use of MT in the classroom, this book offers you new ways of doing this.

- The juxtapositioning of two languages provides opportunities to develop linguistic awareness of the metaphorical, grammatical, phonological, prosodic, lexical and collocational aspects English and MT.

- In multilingual as well as monolingual classes, there is greater scope for developing student autonomy.

- Including MT allows maximum use of limited linguistic resources (the students' English or the teacher's knowledge of MT).

## Who is this Book for?

**If you are a native speaker of your students' MT**, then all the activities in this book are for you.

**If you are a native speaker of English with advanced knowledge of your students' MT**, you will find the whole book open to you.

**If you are a native speaker of English, with a working knowledge of the students' MT, teaching monolingual classes**, you need only be shy of a minority of the activities. The headings 'working knowledge' and 'monolingual' in the summary box at the beginning of the activity indicate this.

**If you are a native speaker of English, teaching multinational classes, or a monolingual class whose language you don't know**, you will be able to use the activities labelled 'zero knowledge' and / or 'multilingual' in the summary box. These activities work on the assumption that you are happy to allow the students **full autonomy** in the work using their MT. Sheelagh and Mario have often worked this way in their own multinational classes.

**If you teach languages other than English**, we should point out that *Using the Mother Tongue* is published by an EFL publisher and in the text we refer to the target language as English. However, the overwhelming majority of the activities would work just as well in a Deutsch als Fremdsprache (DaF), Français Langue Étrangère (FLE) or Chinese as a Foreign Language classroom. We very much hope that teachers of many different languages will find this book a boon.

# What is in this Book?

Most teacher resource books and photocopiables offer ready-made activities that require no preparation. There are plenty of neat and well-cooked activities in this book. There are, however, a number of activities that require some preparation related to the students' MT.

## 1 Organisation

This book is divided into Part A and Part B. The sections in Part A deal with aspects of classroom management. The sections in Part B contain activities that use MT to work on different areas of language.

## Part A: Classroom Management

These three sections look at the ways that MT can be used to create a safe and cooperative working environment.

**Section 1** includes activities designed to set the parameters for the use of MT in class.

**Section 2** shows how MT can be used to encourage cooperation in new groups.

**Section 3** looks at bilingual ways of getting on-going feedback from the students. This is something that we believe is central to student-centred teaching.

## Part B: Living Language

These four sections focus on different areas of language and include activities that use MT to enhance the students' awareness of how English and MT work.

**Section 1** will add substantially to your grammar teaching repertoire, providing you with activities that contrast English and the students' MT.

**Section 2** deals with teaching words and is packed with short activities that you can easily fit into your present way of doing things.

**Section 3** deals with Input, listening and reading, where this book's bilingual focus really comes into its own, speeding up the students' learning process.

**Section 4** deals with Output, speaking and writing, where the use of MT gives students the confidence to produce texts that would otherwise be beyond their level.

**Section 5** looks at ways of using translation. This section will also be of direct use to people who teach translation as a skill in its own right.

## 2 Headings

At the beginning of each activity there is a summary box with headings for the teacher, type of class, level of class, and purpose.

**Teacher** We have chosen three categories for the teacher: zero knowledge of MT, working knowledge of MT and full knowledge of MT. Our understanding of zero knowledge is that we as teachers do know all sorts of things about our student's language even if we can't speak or understand it. Their English gives us that information.

**Class** Many of the activities are suitable for multilingual as well as monolingual classes.

# Feedback and Other Ideas

If you want to contact us about anything in this book, our e-mail addresses are:

Sheelagh Deller: c/o Postmaster@pilgrims.co.uk
Mario Rinvolucri: mario@pilgrims.co.uk

If you have bright bilingual ideas of your own that you would like to share with others, write them up as an article for either:

ENGLISH TEACHING *professional*
etp@etprofessional.com
or
*Humanising Language Teaching*
www.hltmag.co.uk

# 1
# Advocating and Avoiding Mother Tongue

One the problems with group work in monolingual groups is that students may revert to the mother tongue. However, this is not a reason to avoid group work. In group work, we as teachers lose control, so we must give this control to the group. The following questionnaires, activities and strategies could be a useful way of leading you and your students into the activities in this book.

# My Language, the Other Language

| Teacher | working knowledge of students' MT |
|---|---|
| Class | monolingual |
| Level | beginner to advanced |
| Purpose | to encourage students to think about the pluses and minuses of both languages |

## Preparation
For lower levels, translate – or get someone else to translate – the statements into MT.

**1** Dictate the statements 1 to 5. Complete them with the appropriate language. For lower levels, dictate them all in MT.

**2** Tell students to write the sentences and then tick the ones they agree with.

**3** Put the students into groups of about four to compare their feelings.

**4** Ask the groups to add another statement comparing the two languages. Get them to dictate their statement to the rest of the class who raise their hands if they agree with the statement. They can do this in English or MT, depending on level.

**5** If appropriate, continue the dictation with the sentences 6 to 10.

**6** Read out all the sentences again and ask students to raise their hands when you say a sentence they agree with.

---

**My Language, the Other Language Questionnaire**

1  I like the sound of English better than ...

2  I think the tenses in English are more complicated than in ...

3  English is spoken in many more countries than ...

4  The prepositions in English are much more difficult than in ...

5  It's more difficult to guess the pronunciation of words English than in ...

6  English is used much more on the Internet than ...

7  It's easier to ask questions in ... than in English.

8  There are fewer verb endings in English than in ...

9  The numbers in English are easier than in ...

10  There are fewer sounds in English than in ...

# My Mother Tongue / English Process

| Teacher | working knowledge of students' MT |
|---|---|
| Class | monolingual |
| Level | beginner to advanced |
| Purpose | to foster students' awareness of the role MT plays in their use of English |

## Preparation

For lower levels, translate the questionnaire opposite.

**1** In a lower level class dictate the MT translation of the questionnaire. If the class is higher level, dictate the questions in English.

**2** Put the students into small groups to share their answers to the questions.

**Acknowledgement:** The idea of process dictation is widely used in *Ways of Doing* (Davis et al., Cambridge, 1999).

**My Mother Tongue / English Process Questionnaire**

1 How much do I translate inwardly when some one is speaking to me in English?

2 As I read a text in English, do the ideas go straight into my mind or do they come via my mother tongue?

3 If I compare English with other foreign languages that I speak, do I do more or less translation in my head?

4 When I am speaking to some one in English, do my thoughts go **straight** into English or do some of them go via my mother tongue?

5 When I am translating in my head do I hear the words, see the words, or both?

6 When I write English, what happens in my head?

Now write two questions to yourself of your own.

7

8

9 We nearly all talk to ourselves in our heads in mother tongue. Do I ever talk to myself, or to others in my head, in English?

10 I am reading an English text – there is an unknown word – do I want an English definition of the word or do I need an accurate translation into mother tongue?

11 When I write words down in my vocabulary book, do I write the mother tongue first and the English word second?

12 How much have I translated into my mother tongue during this dictation?

*(Only use this question if dictation is given in English.)*

# Mother Tongue Scribe

| | |
|---|---|
| **Teacher** | working knowledge of students' MT |
| **Class** | monolingual |
| **Level** | beginner to advanced |
| **Purpose** | to discourage unnecessary use of MT |
| | to diagnose students' gaps |

Use this activity when you have monolingual groups doing group work.

**1** Choose one member of each group to be the MT scribe. It could be a good idea to ask a student who is particularly prone to using the MT to carry out this task. Or, it could be a lower level student who may have problems with the task. The important thing is that it is not always the same person.

**2** Tell the MT scribe to make a note of anything said in MT. They do **not** note who said it.

**3** At the end of the group work, ask the scribe to give their notes to you.

## Consequences

• Often if the teacher reads out the MT that was used, the students can in fact supply the English. This makes them realise that they are sometimes resorting to MT when it isn't necessary.

• There will probably be some language that they cannot translate back into English. This gives the teacher useful information about language that needs to be worked on.

• The very fact someone is noting down the MT that is spoken can act as a reminder to the group and therefore discourage them from using MT.

• The MT scribe may well find themselves translating as they are writing.

# Mother Tongue Alarm Bells

| | |
|---|---|
| **Teacher** | zero knowledge of students' MT |
| **Class** | monolingual |
| **Level** | beginner to advanced |
| **Purpose** | to deter students from using MT by making them think before they speak |

The following strategies can be used with any kind of activity and should be explained / agreed with the students before the activity starts.

- There is something in the class that the students have to hold if they want to speak in MT. This could be anything: a stone, a dictionary, a piece of chalk, a card.

- There is somewhere in the class they have to be if they want to use MT: in front of the window, for example.

- There is something they have to do if they want to use MT: fold their arms, or point to the ceiling, for example.

- There is something in the class they have to collect if they want to speak MT: paper clips, for example. At the end of the lesson it will be interesting for them to count how many they have accumulated. This may motivate them to collect fewer the next lesson!

- There is something they have to say before they use MT. For example:

  I'm going to use X (their MT) because ...

- Both in class work and when students are working in groups, give them an extra chair – the MT chair. They can only speak in the MT if they sit on that chair, and they are only allowed to sit on it a limited number of times – depending on the difficulty and length of the task.

- For some group work, it may be effective to allocate a limited time when they are allowed to use MT, after which the activity must be in English. This could well be at the beginning so that they can discuss the instructions and plan their strategy. It also enables them to release any initial strong emotions which they may not be able to do in English.

# 2
# Starting New Groups

Working with new groups and getting them to work supportively and effectively together is a crucial part of our teaching. It can affect everything that follows.

At lower levels, this means carrying out some group-formation activities in mother tongue. The fact that lower-level students may not be able to do these activities in English sometimes means that language teachers neglect this important step. However, helping new groups to work with each other, and with us, is essential whatever subject we're teaching. For this reason, we feel that it is sensible to do these activities in mother tongue rather than not at all.

The following activities have been written for low levels, using mother tongue or a mixture of mother tongue and English. However, all the activities can be used with higher-level groups in English, in which case the class could be multilingual and it is not necessary for the teacher to know the students' mother tongues. This is why the suggested levels often range from beginner to much higher levels, depending on which language the students use. The purpose of these activities is to create an effective learning environment rather than work on language.

# Name Groups

| | |
|---|---|
| **Teacher** | zero knowledge of students' MT |
| **Class** | monolingual / multilingual |
| **Level** | beginner to advanced |
| **Purpose** | to make introductions<br>to learn new names |

**1** Ask the students to get into groups with people whose first name starts with the same letter as theirs. To do this, they need space to move around saying their name so they can get together with the other people in their group. The people who end up alone – no one else has a name beginning with their letter – get together in one group.

**2** Once in their groups, get the students to introduce themselves to each other in MT. The purpose here is to learn names without having to focus on new language.

**3** Write 'I'm ...' on the board.

**4** Ask the students in each group to introduce themselves to the whole class, this time in English.

**5** Now ask the students to get into new groups according to how many letters they have in their name. They move around saying the number of letters – in English!

**6** The students introduce themselves to each other in English, using 'I'm ...'

**7** Write 'This is ...' on the board.

**8** Ask the students to repeat the introductions, introducing each other to the whole class in English.

# Miming Introductions

| | |
|---|---|
| **Teacher** | working knowledge of students' MT |
| **Class** | monolingual / multilingual classes<br>(at least 2 students per language) |
| **Level** | elementary to advanced |
| **Purpose** | to use MT for new students to get to know each other |
| **Materials** | dictionaries (optional), sheets of paper |

**1** Put the students into pairs. In multilingual classes, put them into monolingual pairs.

**2** Tell the students that they are going to mime information about themselves to each other. For example, they might mime that they play the piano. Give them a minute to plan what they are going to mime.

**3** One student starts. Their partner has to guess what they are doing and when they guess correctly, they write it down in MT so that they end up with a written list of all the information. Then they change roles.

**4** Students then work together, rewriting the lists of information in English. They can use a dictionary or ask you (by miming it) if they need help. Go round, checking and helping as necessary.

**5** Ask the students to repeat their mimes to each other, this time with their partner describing the action in English. For example:

    play the piano

**6** Put the pairs together to form groups of four. Each student in each pair gives the information about their partner in English. The language used can range in difficulty according to the level of the students. For example:

    play the piano
    He plays the piano.

# Things in Common

| Teacher | working knowledge of students' MT |
|---|---|
| Class | monolingual / multilingual (at least 2 students per language) |
| Level | elementary to advanced |
| Purpose | to use MT for new students to get to know each other |
| Materials | dictionaries (optional) |

**1** Put the students into groups. In multilingual classes, put them into monolingual groups. Tell the students they can speak in MT to find as many things as possible that they have in common. For example, they all have a brother. Ask them to write a list. Give them a time limit of about ten minutes to do this.

**2** Ask the students to translate their list into English. They can use a dictionary or send a messenger to ask you, in order to check.

**3** Ask each group to read out their list in MT and English to the other groups. The other groups listen and clap their hands if they hear anything that is also on their list. This encourages the students to listen.

## Extension
The students could go through their lists a second time, miming the items and getting the rest of the class to say what they are in English.

# Guess What I Did in the Holidays

| Teacher | working knowledge of students' MT |
|---|---|
| Class | monolingual |
| Level | beginner to advanced |
| Purpose | to use MT to enable students to discuss the time they have spent apart |

## Preparation
Write a list of prompts to get students started. Do this in MT or English, depending on the level. For example:

something they bought during the holidays
how often they surfed the Internet
how many CDs they bought
the worst thing they saw on television
a film they watched
a book they read
the most exciting thing they did
a new place they visited
the best meal they ate
what physical exercise they had
the worst day they had

**1** Put your students into pairs, preferably with someone they haven't seen during the holidays. Tell them you are going to read out some questions and they are going to have to guess relevant information about their partner (i.e., they will not be allowed to talk to them).

**2** Dictate the information you prepared. Do this in MT or English, depending on the level. Students guess and write the answers without talking or communicating with each other. Give them time between each item to think of their answer.

**3** When the students have finished writing, let them tell each other what they have written and give each other the correct answers. At lower levels they can do this in MT.

NOTE: The main purpose of this activity is to enable groups to come together and have the opportunity to talk about themselves and find out about each other. Low level students will have to do this activity in MT. The students who are able to do this activity in English will be using the past tense.

# Class Survey

| Teacher | working knowledge of students' MT |
|---|---|
| Class | monolingual |
| Level | elementary to advanced |
| Purpose | to use MT to find out what the students have in common |
| | to work on quantifiers |
| Materials | strips of paper |

## Preparation

Write a number of statements in MT and in English such as the ones below. They should all start with quantifiers. Put each statement on a separate slip of paper. In small classes (i.e., ten students or less), write one sentence for each student. In larger classes, write the same sentence for two or three students.

> All of us have got a brother.
> Most of us are an only child.
> Some of us walk to school.
> None of us have been to England.
> A few of us play a musical instrument.
> All of us surf the web.
> None of us have a PlayStation.
> Some of us like football.
> None of us are vegetarian.
> Most of us find English easy.

**1** Give each student a sentence. In a class of ten, the students can each have a different sentence. If you have a class of thirty, give groups of three students the same sentence. Ask them to read and discuss their sentence and decide if it is true for them.

**2** Divide the class into groups. If three students have the same statement, divide the class into three groups, with one of the students in each group. If two students have the same statement, divide the class into two groups.

**3** Tell your students to find out if their statement is true for their group. For example, if their sentence is 'All of us have got a brother.', they go round asking each other a relevant question such as, 'Have you got a brother?' Depending on the students' level, they can do this in MT or in English. Tell them to keep a record of the answers.

**4** When the students have asked their questions, ask them to use the answers to rewrite the statement so that it is true for the group. If more than one student has been using the same statement, they have to work together to collate their answers.

**5** Ask the students to read out their statements, starting with the one you gave them and then changing it, where necessary, to a statement that is true for the group. For example:

**Original statement**
All of us have got a brother.

**New statement**
In our group, a few of us have got a brother.

**6** If the students are using MT, write the true statements on the board in English. Students copy them into their notebooks.

**NOTE:** This procedure could be used for other purposes, for example, to find out how students like to learn or to get feedback.

# How I Like to Learn

| Teacher | working knowledge of students' MT |
|---|---|
| **Class** | monolingual |
| **Level** | beginner to advanced |
| **Purpose** | to use MT to discover how students like to operate in class |

## Preparation

Write twenty sentences both in MT and in English that will help you discover your students' learning preferences. Below are some examples. The first sentence is designed to show you whether or not the students have understood the instructions.

1  I am a boy / man.

2  I like to work with different partners.

3  I need time to think.

4  I like pair work.

5  I love listening to stories.

6  It helps me to know the equivalent of an English word in my language.

7  I get bored if I have to sit still for too long.

8  I like drawing.

9  I find listening to cassettes difficult.

10  I prefer to sit near the back of the class.

11  I like surfing the net.

12  I find it helpful to read the transcript while listening.

13  I don't like doing group work.

14  I find it difficult to remember new words.

15  English is one of my favourite subjects.

16  I prefer listening to speaking.

17  I don't like it when the teacher corrects me while I'm talking.

18  I like to write new words and phrases in a special book.

19  I like working alone.

20  I never use English outside the classroom.

**1** Tell your students they are going to do a dictation with a difference. You are going to dictate some sentences, but they should only write the sentences that are true for them.

**2** Dictate the sentences in MT.

**3** Read out the sentences again, but this time in MT and in English. Ask the students to raise their hands if they wrote this sentence. Count the hands and make a note of the number of students who wrote each one.

**4** If appropriate, you could read out the sentences another time, this time only in English. Ask the students to raise their hands again if they wrote this sentence.

# Negotiating Ground Rules

| | |
|---|---|
| **Teacher** | working knowledge of students' MT |
| **Class** | monolingual |
| **Level** | elementary to advanced |
| **Purpose** | to use MT to create an effective learning environment |

## Preparation
Make a list of ground rules for class behaviour that are important for you.

**1** On the board, or on two posters, write the headings:

    **It's OK to ...**          **It's not OK to ...**

**2** Invite the students to come up to the board and write in either column. They can do this in a mixture of MT and English. This step works best if you stand at the back of the class so that you are not between them and the board. For example:

| It's OK to ... | It's not OK to ... |
|---|---|
| ask questions | laugh at people |
| have fun | not to listen to others |
| make suggestions | interrupt |
| make mistakes | be late |

**3** It is important not to rush this stage. When there is a pause, allow time for the students to think before bringing the activity to a close.

**4** Add any other points from your prepared list.

**5** Translate any of the items that are written in MT into English.

**6** Ask the students to write out the final version in their notebooks so they can refer to it whenever necessary. They can do this in MT and / or in English.

**7** Negotiate and discuss what is there in MT.

**NOTE:** Sometimes the same item may appear on both sides. For example:

    It's OK to speak Italian.
    It's not OK to speak Italian.

Now is the opportunity to discuss this and, if appropriate, for you to give your opinion or decision. The advantage of this student-generated 'contract' is that students then tend to monitor it for themselves.

# 3
# Getting On-going Feedback

At all levels students probably have information they would like to give us about our lessons and their learning. And from our point of view as teachers, we often need to stop guessing and find out more specifically how the students are feeling and what difficulties they may be experiencing, so that we can respond more closely to their needs.

However, getting feedback is not necessarily a regular occurrence in many classrooms. It is a good idea to ask for feedback from our students regularly, as well as at times when we have a particular question in our heads that we need them to answer.

The activities in this section are multi-purpose. As well as getting feedback, they all practise a particular language area or skill. For example, students may have to listen, do a dictation or use a particular tense.

It is often difficult for students to verbalise feedback in English. If we use mother tongue and English, or only mother tongue, it allows feedback to happen at lower levels. The feedback activities in this section can be done in mother tongue, English or a mixture, depending on the level of the students. All these activities can be used with higher-level groups using English, in which case the class could be multilingual and it is not necessary for the teacher to know the students' mother tongues.

# Head Sentences

| | |
|---|---|
| **Teacher** | working knowledge of students' MT |
| **Class** | monolingual |
| **Level** | beginner to advanced |
| **Purpose** | to encourage students to reflect on their learning<br>to give the teacher useful feedback |
| **Materials** | sheets of paper |

## Preparation

Write about ten sentence stems in MT such as the ones below.

1 I liked ... because ...
2 I'm not sure about ...
3 I didn't like ... because ...
4 I hope ...
5 I'd like to spend more time on ...
6 I'd like to spend less time on ...
7 At the moment I'm feeling ...
8 The most useful thing I've learnt is ...
9 If I was the teacher I'd ...
10 I've decided ...

**1** Write the sentences on the board and ask the students to copy them.

**2** Tell the students that they need to complete the sentences so that they are true for them. However, they should only complete the ones where they really have something to say. Students complete their choice of sentences both in MT and English. At lower levels they may only use MT.

**3** If you want the feedback to be just between you and the students, take in their papers and make a note of their comments.

**4** If you want the students to share the feedback with each other, they can read out their endings. Depending on the level, they can read their sentences in MT or in English.

This step works best if the students all read out their endings to the first sentence and then move on to the second, and so on. Students who haven't completed a sentence just say 'pass'.

**NOTE:** To make the activity more linguistically active, you could add a translation phase. Students read out their sentence in MT and then, as a class, they translate the sentence into English. The final version is written on the board.

# Things I Find Difficult

| | |
|---|---|
| **Teacher** | working knowledge of students' MT |
| **Class** | monolingual |
| **Level** | beginner to advanced |
| **Purpose** | to use MT to encourage students to reflect on why they find things difficult<br>to give the teacher useful feedback<br>to practise giving reasons |

## Preparation

Write some sentences in MT and in English to help your students reflect on their learning. For example:

1 I didn't like the topic.
2 I was tired when we studied it.
3 I didn't concentrate that day.
4 We don't say it like that in my language.
5 The material wasn't clear.
6 The material wasn't interesting.
7 I don't think this item is very important.
8 I don't like the way English does this.

**1** Brainstorm with the students the areas you have been working on in the last month or so. Write the items on the board. This can be done in MT.

**2** Ask the students to look at their list and identify the items they have had most trouble with.

**3** Put your prepared sentences in MT and English on the board. The students use the sentences to help them work out why they had trouble and why certain things were more difficult to learn than others.

**4** Ask the students to read the sentences and say which ones that are true for them.

**5** In pairs, they talk about their answers and write an action plan to help them overcome their difficulties. For example:

● They find an exercise in their books that will help.
● They prepare questions to ask the teacher if something isn't clear.
● They ask another student to help them with a particular confusion.

At lower levels, they do this in MT.

**NOTE:** This is an obvious way to encourage students to take more responsibility for their learning and to become more socially autonomous.

# Circle Your Words

| Teacher | working knowledge of students' MT |
|---|---|
| Class | monolingual |
| Level | beginner to advanced |
| Purpose | to use MT to give the teacher feedback about the mood of the class<br>to help students express their feelings<br>to learn new adjectives |

## Preparation

List a number of adjectives in MT and in English which will give you feedback. For example:

| | | |
|---|---|---|
| fine | all right | too slow |
| fun | too fast | challenging |
| too easy | too difficult | boring |
| interesting | stressful | encouraging |

**1** Write the following heading on the board in MT and in English:

**How do you feel about our lessons?**

**2** Write your prepared list of words on the board in MT.

**3** Ask the students to come to the board and translate any words they can into English.

**4** Give them the English for the words they don't know.

**5** Ask the students to copy the list onto a sheet of paper and circle the words that apply to them.

**6** Ask them to add any other words that are true for them – in MT or in English.

**7** In small groups, get the students to discuss their feelings. Lower levels may do this in MT.

**8** Ask the students to give you their sheets so that you can get an idea of the feelings of the class. These sheets can be anonymous if you think that will make the feedback more honest.

**NOTE:** At beginner level, the entire activity will take place in MT, but the main objective of discovering the mood of the class will still be achieved.

# What Do You Want to Say?

| Teacher | working knowledge of students' MT |
|---|---|
| Class | monolingual |
| Level | beginners to advanced |
| Purpose | to let students direct the feedback to focus on listening |
| Materials | sheets of paper |

**1** Ask the students to write one question about their English lessons that they would like to answer, for example, on a course feedback questionnaire. According to level, this could be in MT or in English. Go round checking their questions if they are in English.

**2** Divide the class into groups of six to twelve.

**3** Distribute sheets of paper.

**4** Tell the students to dictate their questions to the rest of their group. They should write them on their sheet of paper, leaving a space between each for answers. It is important to establish that all questions are valid and that they must not criticise or query anyone else's contribution. Also, if a question is repeated, they should indicate this next to the question.

**5** At this point, you might like to dictate a question that is important to you, in MT or in English.

**6** Give the students time to write their answers individually, then collect them. For lower levels, it would be more effective to ask them to answer the questions in MT.

**NOTE:** The questions the students write give a real insight into their thinking and priorities and provide as much useful feedback as their answers to the questions.

At lower levels the entire activity would be carried out in MT, but the prime objective of getting useful feedback would be achieved.

# Student-generated Dictation

| | |
|---|---|
| **Teacher** | working knowledge of students' MT |
| **Class** | monolingual |
| **Level** | beginner to advanced |
| **Purpose** | to give students the opportunity to give feedback |
| | to give the teacher useful information about the students' feelings |
| | to focus on listening |
| **Materials** | strips of paper |

**1** Ask your students to write down one short sentence in MT on a slip of paper. Tell them this sentence is to give you feedback. You could focus it on one particular area, such as:

> how they are feeling
> what they want to do next
> something they feel confident about
> something they don't feel confident about
> a learning strategy they find helpful
> something they want you to know

In larger classes, put the students into pairs or threes to write a sentence together, so that you don't have more than about twelve sentences.

**2** Collect the slips of paper.

**3** Dictate the sentences in MT. Tell the students only to write down the sentences that are true for them.

**4** Read out the sentences again, but this time say them in English. Ask the students to raise their hands if this is a sentence they have written, so that you can see how many people agree with each sentence. At lower levels, end the activity at this point.

**5** At higher levels, the students then translate all the sentences they have written into English. Ask them to compare notes with other students who have written the same sentences.

**6** Dictate the sentences in English again so that they can listen and check their English versions.

# **Part B** Living Language

# 1
# Grammar

Grammar becomes much less frightening and much more accessible if students are allowed and encouraged to notice the similarities and differences between their own language and English. Mother tongue has a special place when focusing on this.

In this section there are a number of contrastive activities which enable students to focus on the interferences and similarities between their mother tongue and English. Students working on these activities realise that grammar is not just something out there in the foreign language, but is in fact part of their own everyday language.

# Bilingual Sentence Building

| Teacher | working knowledge of students' MT |
|---|---|
| Class | monolingual |
| Level | elementary to advanced |
| Purpose | to make students quickly aware of contrastive grammar |

**1** Tell the students to stand in a circle. If you have a large class, have two or three circles.

**2** Tell them that they will be 'handing' words and phrases round the circle. They pretend the word or phrase they 'pass' to the next person is an object (giving a sense of its weight and temperature, for example). They also say the word loudly and clearly.

If the class MT is French, this is the way the activity might go:

- Student A hands and says a word of their choice to student B: **lapin**
- Student B receives the word and then hands it to student C, translating it: **rabbit**
- Student C receives the word and adds another word: **grey rabbit**
- Student D translates the phrase into MT: **lapin gris**
- Student E adds a word: **viens, lapin gris**
- Student F translates the phrase into English: **come, grey rabbit**
- Student G adds a word: **come here, grey rabbit**
- Student H translates the phrase into French: **viens ici, lapin gris**

**3** Get the words and phrases flowing bilingually round the circles. Stop the students before the sentences get too unwieldy, around ten to twelve words long.

**4** Put the students into pairs and ask them to reconstruct the bilingual sequence in their notebooks.

**NOTE:** This is a linguistic spontaneity activity, so you can't pre-plan the sequences.

# Contrastive Drill

| Teacher | working knowledge of students' MT |
|---|---|
| Class | monolingual |
| Level | elementary to advanced |
| Purpose | to focus on a specific MT / English contrast |
| Materials | copies of exercise |

## Preparation
Choose a written exercise to practise a language point that is difficult for the students, for example, one where there is MT interference. This could be from the coursebook. For example:

**To contrast 'of' and 'from'**
This book was a present _____ my sister.
It's a long way _____ Rio to Buenos Aires.
We still haven't received that payment _____ BMW.
It's in the north _____ Germany.

**1** Ask the students to complete the exercise. When everyone has finished, go through the answers with the whole class.

**2** Then go round the class as follows:

- Student A translates and reads out the first sentence in MT.
- Student B translates it back into English.
- Student B translates and reads out the second sentence in MT.
- Student C translates it back into English.

**3** Continue this process until everyone has had a turn. Alternatively, do this step in pairs or small groups.

# Contrasting Tenses or Structures

| | |
|---|---|
| **Teacher** | working knowledge of students' MT |
| **Class** | monolingual |
| **Level** | lower intermediate to advanced |
| **Purpose** | to help students distinguish between two often-confused English grammar structures by translating them into MT |
| **Materials** | sheets of paper |

## Preparation

Write four pairs of sentences or phrases in English which contain contrasting structures. See below for some examples. Write each pair of sentences on a separate sheet of paper.

I've been living here all my life.
I lived there for ten years.

I haven't been going out much lately.
I went out every Friday night last month.

We've been seeing too much of those two.
We saw them coming up the hill.

Have you been waiting long?
Did you wait until the end?

Hasn't she been skating yet?
Did she go skating with you?

He's been talking about his bad luck again.
He talked to them about photography.

We've gone there three times so far.
We went there after work.

She's started learning English five times.
She started her course last month.

You've wanted one of these for ages.
You wanted a big red one.

Haven't you called her?
Didn't you call her?

Hasn't he told you the news?
Didn't he tell you the news?

**1** Put the students into groups of four and give each member one sheet with one of the pairs of sentences at the top.

**2** Ask the students to read their sentences and check that they understand them.

**3** Students translate their two sentences from English into MT, leaving a generous space between the original and the translated versions.

**4** When the students have finished translating, ask them to fold their sheet over so that only the translation is visible and pass it to another member of their group.

**5** Ask this student then to translate the sentences back from MT into English.

**6** Get the students to compare the translations and discuss the problems they have in distinguishing between the pairs.

**NOTE:** Students can write their own sets of pairs in class or as homework. Check for accuracy and also make sure that the pairs are contrasting the structures you are working on, before continuing with the activity.

**Acknowledgement:** We learnt this activity from Tim Hahn.

# Contrastive Grammar Recognition

| Teacher | full knowledge of students' MT |
|---|---|
| Class | monolingual |
| Level | elementary |
| Purpose | to help students become aware of how English works compared to their MT |
| Materials | copies of text |

## Preparation
Translate the text below. Make copies of the English and the MT translation.

**1** Give out both versions of the text to each student. In the MT translation, ask them to underline all the words that match the capitalised parts of the English version (equivalencies). For example:

**English:** | **French:**
So, DID (1) you get ... | Est-ce-que tu as reçu ...

**2** Put the students into groups of four and ask them to compare their underlinings. Tell them they can ask questions about anything they don't understand.

**3** Answer their questions and focus their minds on one bit of the grammar explored.

---

**Contrastive Grammar Recognition Text**
**A:** Happy Christmas, John.
**B:** Hi, Pa.
**A:** Well, (1) DID you get what I sent you?
**B:** (2) YEP. Thanks.
**A:** Well, what (3) DO you think? The people in the shop told me it was the (4) VERY latest model ...
**B:** It's well good, but ...
**A:** But what, exactly?
**B:** You see, I'm not (4) INTO Action Men right now. I mean, I (5) USED to be ...
**A:** Perhaps we could return it to the place I bought it.
**B:** (6) DO THAT.
**A:** So, (7) HOW's it going?
**B:** OK.
**A:** (8) HOW's school?
**B:** Fine.

---

**NOTE:** The intellectual focus on the contrast between the two language occupies the students' conscious attention. In the meantime, they unconsciously absorb chunks of language.

This technique is one you can add to your repertoire of ways you treat coursebook dialogues or reading texts.

**Acknowledgement:** We learnt this idea from Peter Wilberg, writing in *Humanising Language Teaching*, Year 2 Issue 2, April 1999. To read his article, 'Interlingual Training Technology', go to: www.htlmag.co.uk and look under 'Major Article'.

# Students Help Each Other

| Teacher | full knowledge of students' MT |
|---|---|
| Class | monolingual |
| Level | elementary |
| Purpose | to use MT to allow lower levels to do a higher level activity |
| | to work on interrogative patterns, in present and past simple |
| Materials | OHP / sheet of A3 paper |

## Preparation

There are two ways of doing this activity. In this example you need to 'borrow' a couple of higher level 'guest' students from one of your colleagues' classes for the duration of your lesson. If you cannot 'borrow' students, see the Variation below.

**1** Tell the group this mystery story in English:

> The first person spoke.
> There was a pause.
> The second person spoke.
> Then the third person got up and slapped the first person in the face.

**2** Tell the same story again in the students' MT.

**3** Tell it again in English and write it on the board.

**4** Explain to the students, in MT, that they are going to ask you questions in English or MT to find out why the third person hit the first person in the face. They must ask 'yes' / 'no' questions, as you will only answer 'yes' or 'no'.

**5** When a student asks a question in MT, the first guest student should silently write it on the board in English. The questioner then repeats their question in English before you answer.

**6** The second guest student should write down all the questions on an OHP transparency or A3 sheet.

**7** Once the students have found the solution (you may have to give them clues, for example, 'focus on the second person'), clean the board and ask the second guest student to dictate all the questions the group has asked. They then put up the transparency so the students can check.

> (A good solution to the puzzle above is that the second man was an interpreter, but accept any other logical endings eg: number 2 was a Mafia boss and number 3 was his bodyguard.)

**NOTE:** Using the higher level students to translate allows the class to do a lower intermediate problem-solving exercise while they are below the linguistic level. Using translation makes the work pleasurable and efficient. It allows the group to cope with quite a lot of text in English, most of it their own, and all of it intensely structure-loaded. On-the-spot interpretation is also demanding language practice for the advanced students.

## Variation

Prepare one of the students in your class to act as question-answerer, making sure this person fully understands the story and its solution. You interpret from MT to English and note all the questions asked. You give the dictation at the end.

**NOTE:** For more puzzle stories, see Appendix (page 95) and *Challenge to Think* (Berer et al., Oxford, 1982). The teacher's book gives the stories on page 6 and the solutions on page 85.

Also see Paul Sloane's list of Lateral Thinking Puzzles at: <http://einstein.et.tudelft.nl/~arlet/puzzles/lateral.html>

# Correction Exercise

| Teacher | working knowledge of students' MT |
|---------|-----------------------------------|
| Class | monolingual |
| Level | elementary to advanced |
| Purpose | to focus on MT interference |

## Preparation

Identify the student errors you want to work on. Write a correct sentence in English for each error.

**1** Dictate the sentences in English, but ask the students to write them only in MT.

**2** Put the students into pairs and ask them to compare their MT sentences. For example:

| | |
|---|---|
| **Problem:** | before to start |
| **Dictated sentence:** | Before starting, I want to go over what we did last time. |
| **Student's sentence:** | Avant de commencer je voudrais ... |

**3** Ask them to translate their sentences back into English.

# Loud and Soft

| Teacher | working knowledge of students' MT |
|---------|-----------------------------------|
| Class | monolingual |
| Level | elementary to lower intermediate |
| Purpose | to focus attention on the contrast between a structure in English and in MT |

## Preparation

Choose a passage from your coursebook that you want your students to revise. Underline all the occurrences of the structure.

**1** Tell the class you are going to dictate a text to them. When you speak normally, they write the words in English; when you whisper, they write in MT.

**2** When giving the dictation, whisper the underlined structure words you want them to focus on and to translate into MT.

**3** Get several students to read their texts back, but all in English.

# Student-student Tests

| Teacher | working knowledge of students' MT |
|---------|-----------------------------------|
| Class | monolingual |
| Level | lower intermediate to advanced |
| Purpose | to focus on MT interference |
| Materials | sheets of paper |

## Preparation

Choose four or five language points you want your students to work on. Focus on areas where there is MT interference, such as: use of tense; word order; syntax; false friends.

**1** Put the students into groups of four. Give each group a different language point and tell them that you want them to write a test on it.

**2** Ask each group to write about six sentences to illustrate their specific language point. They should write the sentences in English and then translate them into MT on a separate sheet of paper. For example:

> **To test 'for' and 'since'**
> We've been doing this for ages.
> We've had this book since September.
> We've been learning English since we were twelve.
>
> (The MT translations would be on a separate sheet of paper.)

**3** Check their sentences.

**4** Ask the groups to exchange their MT sentences and translate them into English.

**5** Tell them to give their English sentences back to the group who wrote them. These students then correct the sentences.

# Student-generated Multiple Choice

| Teacher | full knowledge of students' MT |
|---|---|
| Class | monolingual |
| Level | upper intermediate to advanced |
| Purpose | to raise contrastive awareness between English and MT of two words that are often confused |
| Materials | copies of Translation Worksheet (see page 35) |

## Preparation
Write a number of sentences in English which highlight two words that are often confused. Photocopy the worksheet so that there is one copy per four students. The template on page 35 is designed to highlight the difference between 'as' and 'like'.

**1** Put the students into groups of four. Give out one Translation Worksheet to each group.

**2** Ask the students to work on each sentence and write four translations for each one. They should write three acceptable translations and one that is incorrect.

**3** Tell them to exchange their worksheets with another group. With this worksheet, they should each cross out the incorrect translation and choose the translation they like best for each sentence.

**4** At class level, get the groups to compare their findings.

**NOTE:** Collect in the worksheets, check them and then use them for the next exercise in this book with lower level students. This is a perfect example of a student-generated exercise that is then used by other students.

**LANGUAGE NOTE:** the meanings of 'as' and 'like' (in the worksheet on page 35) are based on the senses and examples given in the *Collins COBUILD Dictionary* (Collins Cobuild, 1987). Both have several more meanings than the ones given above. You can easily put together Translation Worksheets for areas where your students have difficulties. You might get your students working on areas like:

some / any   for / since   such / so

# Grammar Translation Multiple Choice

| Teacher | full knowledge of students' MT |
|---|---|
| Class | monolingual |
| Level | lower to upper intermediate |
| Purpose | to raise contrastive awareness between English and MT of two words that are often confused |
| Materials | copies of Translation Worksheets |

## Preparation
There are two ways of preparing for this activity. The easiest way is to use translation worksheets produced by your higher-level students as with *Student-generated Multiple Choice*. Alternatively, prepare your own Translation Worksheet. Write a number of sentences in English that highlight two English words that are often confused. Add four translations for each sentence, one of which is incorrect. Photocopy your Translation Worksheet so that there is one copy per pair of students. For example, to contrast 'as' / 'like' where the students' MT is French you could write:

She wept bitterly as she told her story.
a) Elle pleura amèrement, tout en racontant son histoire.
b) Comme elle raconta son histoire, elle pleura amèrement.
c) Elle pleura amèrement tandis qu'elle racontait son histoire.
d) Elle pleurait amèrement tandis qu'elle racontait son histoire.

**1** Put the students into pairs. Give out one completed Translation Worksheet to each pair.

**2** Ask the students to work on each sentence and cross out the translation that is incorrect. They should then underline the translation they think is the best.

**3** Ask one pair to write up the translations they think are incorrect on the board.

**4** Ask another pair to write up the translations they think are the best on the board.

**5** Allow discussion and only come in yourself if you are sure the whole class is going down a blind alley.

**LANGUAGE NOTE:** See opposite, *Student-generated Multiple Choice*, for other contents and sources.

**1** She wept bitterly as she told her story.

   **a)**

   **b)**

   **c)**

   **d)**

**2** I am as good a cook as she is.

   **a)**

   **b)**

   **c)**

   **d)**

**3** He's like a little baby.

   **a)**

   **b)**

   **c)**

   **d)**

**4** There were as many as 500 balloons.

   **a)**

   **b)**

   **c)**

   **d)**

**5** What does that soup taste like?

   **a)**

   **b)**

   **c)**

   **d)**

**6** She worked as a waitress.

   **a)**

   **b)**

   **c)**

   **d)**

**7** They need a rest. They've been working like crazy.

   **a)**

   **b)**

   **c)**

   **d)**

**8** He was sleeping in the same hotel as I was.

   **a)**

   **b)**

   **c)**

   **d)**

**9** He looked at me as if I were mad.

   **a)**

   **b)**

   **c)**

   **d)**

**10** She left no instructions as to what I should cook.

   **a)**

   **b)**

   **c)**

   **d)**

**11** He won't move for the likes of them.

   **a)**

   **b)**

   **c)**

   **d)**

**12** You've been running sixteen miles a day - that's more like it!

   **a)**

   **b)**

   **c)**

   **d)**

*Using the Mother Tongue* © Sheelagh Deller and Mario Rinvolucri published by ENGLISH TEACHING *professional* and DELTA PUBLISHING

# Grammar Exploration via Translation

| Teacher | working knowledge of students' MT |
|---------|-----------------------------------|
| Class | monolingual |
| Level | beginner to advanced |
| Purpose | to raise awareness of grammar and word order changes as you go from MT to English |

## Preparation

Write up a sentence in the students' MT that, once translated into English, will contain the grammar pattern you are working on.

Suppose English is the group's MT and you are teaching them Japanese, you might write up this sentence in MT:

Japanese people eat rice

The Japanese target sentence is:

| Nihon | jin | wa | gohan | o | tabemasu |
|-------|-----|-----|-------|---|----------|
| Japanese | people | | rice | | eat |

Without showing the students the Japanese sentence, ask them how many words are needed to translate the sentence into Japanese. If fewer words are needed, ask them which words will be dropped. If more words are needed, ask them which words will be added.

The correct number for the Japanese sentence is six words. Ask the class what the two extra words are and where they will go in the sequence:

1    2    3    4    5    6

If possible, elicit that 'wa', the topic marker, is No. 3 and 'o', the object marker, is No. 5. Get a student to come to the board to write the words in under the corresponding numbers.

Elicit the rest of the Japanese sentence. If a student writes up a mistaken word or puts a word in the wrong position, do **not** leap in and correct. Allow time for the group to sort it out themselves. Only intervene if the students are happy to be totally wrong.

**1** Use the above procedure with a sentence in the students' MT that they bring over into English.

**2** Repeat the procedure with several MT sentences that, when translated into English, show the pattern you want the students to work on.

# Grammar Translation Dictation

| Teacher | working knowledge of students' MT |
|---------|-----------------------------------|
| Class | monolingual / multilingual (at least 2 students per language) |
| Level | elementary to advanced |
| Purpose | to focus on a specific grammar difficulty |

## Preparation

Write out some sentences or sentence stems in English, focusing on a specific language difficulty for your students. For example:

**Present Simple or Present Continuous**
I'm sitting next to ...
I'm writing in ... (language)
I live in ...
I go to school by ...
I'm wearing ...
I do my homework in the ...
I often wear ...
The teacher's dictating in ...

**1** Dictate the sentence stems in English.

**2** Ask the students to listen and write the sentences in MT. If they are sentence stems as in the example, the students should complete the sentences so that they are true for them. It's important that they do **not** write the sentences in English. Tell them to leave a space between the sentences.

**3** At the end of the dictation, give the students a chance to compare their MT sentences.

**4** Tell the students to translate each sentence back into English.

**5** Go through the sentences and ask the students to notice how this difference in meaning would be made in MT.

NOTE: This process can be used at higher levels with more difficult content.

# Two Language Dictogloss

| | |
|---|---|
| **Teacher** | full knowledge of students' MT |
| **Class** | monolingual |
| **Level** | upper intermediate to advanced |
| **Purpose** | to use input in MT and English to help students reconstruct a complex sentence |

## Preparation

Choose a complex, embedded sentence in English that is appropriate for the level of your students. For example:

> Though Charles liked to think of himself as a scientific young man and would probably not have been too surprised had news reached him out of the future of the aeroplane, the jet engine, television, radar: what **would** have astounded him was the changed attitude to time itself.
>
> *The French Lieutenant's Woman*, John Fowles (Jonathan Cape, 1969)

Translate it into the students' MT. The first time round, it is better to choose a sentence that is too easy rather than one that is too difficult.

**1** Tell the students that they are going to be doing a sentence reconstruction exercise, going from MT into English. Their aim is to produce a word-perfect reconstruction.

**2** Read the sentence to them in MT. Pause for a while. Read the sentence to them in English. Pause. Read the sentence to them in MT.

**3** Put the students into pairs and ask them to reconstruct the sentence in English.

**4** Ask one student to go to the board and work as scribe while the others dictate their version.

**5** Finally, give the English sentence to one of the students to read out so that the scribe can correct what is on the board.

**6** Allow feedback time so that the students can explore the language processes they went though in order to do the exercise.

**NOTE:** Apart from reading the sentences clearly and convincingly, your role is to keep out of the activity. It is a useful moment to observe the group.

# If I Could Speak English ...

| | |
|---|---|
| **Teacher** | zero knowledge of students' MT |
| **Class** | monolingual |
| **Level** | lower intermediate to advanced |
| **Purpose** | to raise contrastive awareness between MT and English<br>to work on hypothetical 'if' clauses |
| **Materials** | sheets of paper |

**1** Ask each student to write one simple true personal fact in English. For example:

> I have two sisters.

**2** Ask the students to rewrite their sentence starting with 'If':

> If I didn't have two sisters, I'd have my own bedroom.

**3** Put the students into groups of four (A – D). Write the following instructions on the board:

> **Student A:** Dictate your sentence to student B in English.
>
> **Student B:** Put student A's sentence into the third person and dictate to student C.
>
> **Student C:** Translate student B's sentence into MT and dictate to student D.
>
> **Student D:** Translate student C's sentence back into English and dictate to the group.

**4** Tell each student in each group to copy one of the sentences on the board onto a piece of paper and put it on their chair.

**5** Student A dictates their 'If' sentence to student B in English.

**6** Student B transforms the sentence into the third person in English and dictates it to student C. For example:

> If she didn't have two sisters, she'd have her own bedroom.

**7** Student C translates this sentence into MT and dictates it to student D.

**8** Student D translates it back into English and dictates it to the group.

**9** They repeat the process moving round their circle onto the next chair

# 2
# Vocabulary

Mother tongue can be a valuable tool for extending vocabulary. There are a number of ways of revising and activating already-known vocabulary but the introduction of new vocabulary often seems to be left to what arises out of a text. This section offers you lots of ways of actually teaching new vocabulary. Using mother tongue replaces guessing, which can be both time-consuming and inaccurate. The mother tongue also enables students to use words in English that they choose themselves, i.e. words they think of in their mother tongue but don't know in English. Another important use of the mother tongue is for the purpose of collocation, so that students can compare common combinations in their mother tongue that may be different in English.

# From 1 to 20

| Teacher | zero knowledge of students' MT |
|---|---|
| Class | monolingual / multilingual (at least 2 students per language) |
| Level | beginner to lower intermediate |
| Purpose | to help students become agile with numbers |

**1** Put the students into pairs (A and B). In multilingual classes, put them into monolingual pairs.

**2** Explain that in this exercise, student A counts forwards and student B counts backwards.

**3** Demonstrate with two students. For example, with Japanese students this would go:

> **Student A:** ichi, ni, san, shi
> **Student B:** four, three, two, one
> **Student A:** ni, san, shi, go
> **Student B:** five, four, three, two
> **Student A:** san, shi, go, roku
> **Student B:** six, five, four, three

Make sure that they do the counting rhythmically. A hand clap or finger click helps.

**4** Tell the pairs to do the exercise from 1, 2, 3, 4 to 17, 18, 19, 20.

**5** Get the students to repeat the exercise, swapping roles.

# From 10,000 to 50,000

| Teacher | zero knowledge of students' MT |
|---|---|
| Class | monolingual / multilingual (at least 2 students per language) |
| Level | elementary to advanced |
| Purpose | to speed up students' ability to manipulate large numbers |

**1** Put the students into pairs (A and B). In multilingual classes, put them into monolingual pairs.

**2** Explain that student A counts up from 10,000 in MT, adding 1001 each time. Student B counts down from 50,000 in English, subtracting 1001 each time. They each write their numbers as they say them.

**3** Demonstrate with two students. With Spanish students, this would go:

> **Student A:** diez mil
> **Student B:** fifty thousand
> **Student A:** once mil uno
> **Student B:** forty-eight thousand nine hundred and ninety-nine
> **Student A:** doce mil dos
> **Student B:** forty-seven thousand nine hundred and ninety-eight

**4** Tell the pairs to do the exercise.

**5** Get the students to repeat the exercise, swapping roles.

**6** Ask them how they found the exercise and then broaden out the discussion to how they feel about doing number work in English.

**NOTE:** This exercise is useful for all students but it is especially appropriate for speakers of languages from the Confucian part of the world who work in base 10,000. For a Japanese speaker, 26,000 is 'Two **man** (10,000), six thousand'.

**Acknowledgement:** We learnt this activity type from *On Love and Psychological Exercises* (Orage A R, Samuel Weiser, 1988).

# It's on the Tip of My Tongue

| Teacher | full knowledge of students' MT |
| --- | --- |
| Class | monolingual |
| Level | lower to upper intermediate |
| Purpose | to learn body expressions |

## Preparation

Write this gapped list of body expressions on the board.

| Body Expressions | Key |
| --- | --- |
| 1  to put your _____ in it. | foot |
| 2  to cost an _____ and a _____ . | arm / leg |
| 3  to give someone the cold _____ . | shoulder |
| 4  to give someone an _____ful. | ear |
| 5  to give something the _____ up. | thumbs |
| 6  to turn the other _____ . | cheek |
| 7  to twist someone's _____ . | arm |
| 8  to be thick-_____ed. | skin |
| 9  to turn a blind _____ . | eye |
| 10  to be on the tip of your _____ . | tongue |

**1** Call out the following parts of the body and ask your students to touch the matching part of the body as you say the words.

| | | | | |
| --- | --- | --- | --- | --- |
| arm | shoulder | eye | tongue | cheek |
| ear | leg | foot | thumb | skin |

**2** Tell the students to fill in the gaps on the board.

**3** Check their answers at class level and ask them to explain what each expression means.

**4** Put the students into small groups and ask them to write the equivalent expression in MT, using a body word where possible.

**5** Rub out the list on the board.

**6** Get the groups to take it in turns to read out an MT sentence (in random order). The rest of the class should translate it back into English.

**NOTE:** This technique can be used for learning any group of idioms, for example: animals, money, colour, temperature, etc.

# Before Napoleon

| Teacher | full knowledge of students' MT |
| --- | --- |
| Class | monolingual / multilingual (at least 2 students per language) |
| Level | upper intermediate to advanced |
| Purpose | to help students come to grips with UK and US measures |

**1** Put the students into pairs (A and B). In multilingual classes, put them into monolingual pairs.

**2** Tell them you are going to dictate some sentences in English. Student A should write them down in English while student B writes them down in MT. Tell them you will allow time between each item for consultation within the pairs about translation difficulties. Point out that the sentences in English are all related to pre-metric measurements. Make it clear that there may not be an exact equivalence, so they may have to find another way of expressing this in MT.

**3** Dictate the sentences below.

**4** Go through the sentences with the whole class focusing on the problems in the English sentences.

| Non-Metrical Sentences |
| --- |
| 1  The peace talks inched towards their climax. |
| 2  They were travelling at fifty miles an hour. |
| 3  I really can't fathom his motivation. |
| 4  Give her an inch and she'll take a mile. |
| 5  Call the doctor! His temperature's 102. |
| 6  He's down to eight stone and still losing weight. |
| 7  This website is miles better than ours. |
| 8  A miss is as good as a mile. |
| 9  I've still got acres of reading to do. |
| 10  He just managed to lift the piano, using every ounce of strength he possessed. |
| 11  Those tyres run on thirty. |
| 12  Earth calling John ... you were miles away! |
| 13  Anyone with an ounce of intelligence would see that's rubbish. |
| 14  She takes size seven shoes. |

# What's the Verb?

| | |
|---|---|
| **Teacher** | zero knowledge of students' MT |
| **Class** | monolingual / multilingual (at least 2 students per language) |
| **Level** | elementary |
| **Purpose** | to learn and compare verb-noun collocations |
| **Materials** | dictionaries |

**1** Invite the students to come to the board and write the names of sports.

**2** Ask them to write the sports in their books and add a verb in MT to each one which would mean to 'practise' the sport. For example:

> to **play** tennis, to **do** karate

**3** Ask the students to translate the verbs into English with the help of a dictionary.

**NOTE:** This is a very confusing area in English, but it is a high frequency one, so it is worth giving students some guidelines:

- In English we use the verb 'play' for all ball games. For example: 'play football', 'play tennis', 'play basketball'.
- Non-ball games use the verb 'do'. For example: 'do aerobics', 'do karate'. ('darts' is one of the exceptions and uses 'play').
- Sports ending in '-ing' use 'go' or 'do', but 'go' is more usual. For example: 'to go fencing' / 'to do fencing'.

For further linguistic information, see page 991 of *The Longman Language Activator* (Longman, 1993).

Choose any area of verb / noun collocations that are different to the MT. For example: 'make' / 'do', or delexicalised verbs such as 'have'. There are a number of verbs in English which are used both lexically and delexically. For example, the word 'have' has a basic meaning of 'to possess'. It is often used, however, to carry a noun where is does not have its lexical meaning but reflects the meaning of the noun. For example: 'to have a shower', 'to have breakfast'.

# Guess My Word

| | |
|---|---|
| **Teacher** | working knowledge of students' MT |
| **Class** | monolingual / multilingual (at least 2 students per language) |
| **Level** | elementary to advanced |
| **Purpose** | to get students to learn new words in English by using MT to give definitions |
| **Materials** | dictionaries (optional) |

**1** Choose a vocabulary heading appropriate for your class: For example:

> Things that ...  are round
> move
> smell
> live in the sea
> cost more than ...
> hurt
> open and shut

**2** Ask each student to list as many words as they can think of in the category you have chosen. They should write the ones they know in English and the others in MT. Give them a time limit.

**3** Give the students time to translate their MT words into English. (They can ask you / each other or check in a dictionary.)

**4** Put the students into pairs (A and B). In multilingual classes, put the students into monolingual pairs. Tell student A to choose one of their words and describe it as clearly as possible to student B without saying the word itself. At lower levels, this can be done in MT. If student B guesses what the word is, they say the word in English if they can, or if not, in MT. If student B cannot guess, student A should teach them the word in English, and student B make a note of it.

**5** Tell the pairs to swap round, with student B choosing a word from their list.

**6** In monolingual classes, after a few rounds you can ask the students to change partners and repeat the process. Add the rule that if they have just learnt any new English words, they must define these words for their new partner. This will reinforce them.

# Contrasting Collocations

| | |
|---|---|
| **Teacher** | full knowledge of students' MT |
| **Class** | monolingual / multilingual (at least 3 students per language) |
| **Level** | upper intermediate to advanced |
| **Purpose** | to contrastively analyse the words that collocate with 'silent' and 'silence' in English and MT |
| **Materials** | dictionaries (optional) |

**1** Ask the students what sound a parent makes to get silence from a child. In English the sound is 'shhh'. Other languages do this differently.

**2** Ask them to draw three quick sketches of things they associate with 'silence'.

**3** Put the students into groups of three and ask them to whisper explanations of their sketches. In multilingual classes, put students into monolingual groups.

**4** Softly dictate the following phrases, making sure everybody can hear you at the back.

    a threatening silence
    a thoughtful silence
    a silent film
    the guns fell silent
    a rather silent, stand-offish person
    taciturn
    an eerie silence
    reserved
    a silent girl, cool and aloof
    a silent letter
    a hush
    a shocked silence
    silence is golden
    Silent Night, Holy Night
    the silence of the high mountains
    she silenced me with a look
    he's the strong, silent type
    a gun with a silencer
    we can buy his silence
    a smug silence

**5** Speaking in a soft voice, ask the students to work in their groups and check out any spellings and meanings they are not sure of.

**6** Ask each of them to pick out five of the dictated phrases above that they have experienced and to tell their group about each situation. This might be a time when someone experienced an eerie silence, for example.

**7** Ask the groups to look through the list to see if any of the English collocations translate directly into MT.

**8** Ask the groups to find a dozen strong collocates of 'silent' / 'silence' in MT and to translate them into English.

**9** Get the English translations of the collocations from the different groups and write them up on the board.

**NOTE:** This technique can be applied to any collocational field.

Many of the collocations in the dictation above have a negative hue to them. Not all languages hear 'silence' this way and it is interesting when this sort of cultural awareness dawns on students.

# Collocational Networks

| | |
|---|---|
| **Teacher** | full knowledge of students' MT |
| **Class** | monolingual |
| **Level** | upper intermediate to advanced |
| **Purpose** | to raise awareness of the different collocational patterns in MT and English |

## Preparation

Choose some words your students know well. Look each word up in a corpus-based dictionary (see note below) and choose some pre- and post-positional collocations. For example:

**CHOCOLATE**
**pre-positional:** dark, white, plain, melted, hot, drinking, milk, grated
**post-positional:** factory, money, cake, bar

**1** Choose one of the words and dictate just the collocations in English.

**2** Ask the students to write the words you dictate and then decide what English word would collocate with all the words in the list.

**3** Ask them to suggest corresponding MT collocations.

**4** Put the students into groups and give each group one of the words you have prepared. Don't give them the collocations. For example:

| | |
|---|---|
| **relationship** | (stable, close, long-term, stormy, loving, meaningful, deep) |
| **smoker** | (light, heavy, non-, passive, chain, ex-, occasional, pipe) |
| **house** | (dream, full, dolls, period, detached, tree, haunted, town, show, period, summer, coffee) |
| **garden** | (herb, rose, sunken, vegetable, walled) |
| **fish** | (raw, flat, sea, smoked, oily, fresh, frozen, tank, bone, food) |
| **traffic** | (jam, flow, lights, island, warden, sign, light, heavy) |

**5** Tell the students to list all the English words they can think of that collocate with their word.

**6** Tell each group to read out their list and the rest of the class to write the words down. In groups, they decide what the starting word was for the list.

**7** Tell each group to work out how their English collocations would translate into MT.

**8** Tell the groups to read out their MT collocations. The rest of the class should say the English equivalents.

**NOTE:** Useful dictionaries for this purpose are the *Collins COBUILD Dictionary* (Collins Cobuild, 1987), the *Dictionary of Selected Collocations* (LTP, 1997) and the *Oxford Collocations Dictionary* (Oxford, 2002).

# The World of 'Give'

| | |
|---|---|
| **Teacher** | full knowledge of students' MT |
| **Class** | monolingual / multilingual (at least 4 students per language) |
| **Level** | upper intermediate to advanced |
| **Purpose** | to get students to explore the many ways that 'give' can be used |
| **Materials** | OHP / sheet of A3 paper |

## Preparation

Prepare a transparency (or a sheet of A3 paper) with your translations of the 'give' sentences below.

**1** To get the students thinking about the word, write GIVE in the middle of the board and ask a student to come out and work as the scribe. Tell the students to shout out all the phrases they know in English containing the word. The scribe writes them down in disorder all over the board.

**2** Put the students into pairs (A and B). In multilingual classes, put the students into monolingual pairs. Explain that you are going to give a dictation. Student A should write down the sentences in English while student B should write them down in MT.

**3** Dictate the sentences below in English, allowing time for the pairs to consult over the translation.

> They gave us a wonderfully warm welcome.
> Jane gave him a hug.
> He gave him a good kick.
> She gave him a long kiss.
> The poetry professor is required to give a lecture every term.
> They gave me a leaflet.
> My wife gave away my best raincoat.
> It's mine! Give it back!

**4** Tell the pairs to swap so that student B now writes in English and student B translates into MT. Continue the dictation:

> The old world was giving way to the new.
> Absolute rubbish! Don't give me that!
> Give way to the traffic coming from the right.
> We mustn't give in to threats.
> She had to give up her job.
> It's three hundred miles to Edinburgh, give or take ten.
> He was a believer in the give and take of democracy.
> Given the chance, I'd love to go to Bhuttan.

**5** Put the students into groups of four and ask them to compare their translations. Circulate, helping where necessary.

**6** Put your own translations up on the OHP / A3 sheet of paper.

**LANGUAGE NOTE:** The first four sentences are examples of what the *Co-build Grammar* calls 'delexical' verbs. In these utterances 'give' is semantically empty. Most of the other sentences are entries listed under 'give' in the *Collins COBUILD Dictionary* (Collins Cobuild, 1987).

As the dictionary entries are carefully chosen to be the most frequent uses of a given word from the huge Collins computer corpus, you know you are teaching your students language relevant to their level. You will find a similar exercise round the verb 'take' on page 130 of *More Grammar Games* (Davis et al., Cambridge, 1995).

# New Words Galore

| Teacher | working knowledge of students' MT |
|---|---|
| Class | monolingual |
| Level | elementary to advanced |
| Purpose | to use MT for peer teaching |
| Materials | sheets of A3 paper, coloured pens, dictionaries (optional) |

**1** Choose a topic, for example, 'Transport', and write the heading on the board.

**2** Ask the students to brainstorm different sub-areas of the topic. Ask them to write these on the board.

**3** Have a class vote to choose four sub-areas, for example: 'Road', 'Air', 'Sea', 'Rail'.

**4** Put students into four groups, with about six students in each group. For larger classes, have an additional four groups.

**5** Tell each group to appoint a messenger and a scribe. Give each scribe a sheet of A3 paper and a different coloured pen. Explain that the class will need to recognise each group by the colour of the pen they use.

**6** Allocate one of the sub-areas to each group and ask the scribe to write this heading in the middle of the sheet. Explain that it is better for the sheet to be used horizontally.

**7** Set a time limit (for example, two to three minutes) and ask the groups to tell their scribes any words that fit into their sub-area. If they don't know the words in English they should write them in MT. The scribe should scatter these words over the sheet rather than put them into a vertical list.

**8** When the time limit is up, ask the scribes to pass their sheets to the group on their left.

**9** When they receive the new topic from the other group, the scribe should read out the words. Explain that if there are any words that they don't understand, they can send their messenger to ask the group who wrote it for a translation. If there are any words in MT that they can translate into English, they write them next to the MT word. They also send their messenger to tell the original group the translation.

Then they add any more words they can think of in English or MT.

The time limit for this and subsequent rounds will need to be a bit longer, perhaps four minutes.

**10** Repeat this process until the groups get their original sheets back. If at this point there are still words in MT, they translate them by using a dictionary or asking the teacher, and the messenger again goes to the group who wrote the word to give them the translation.

**11** This can be followed up with each group writing out the new words on their sheet and dictating them to the whole class.

# One Word, Many Meanings

| Teacher | full knowledge of students' MT |
|---|---|
| Class | monolingual |
| Level | upper intermediate |
| Purpose | to make students aware of the multiple meanings of an English word |

## Preparation

Choose a word that has more than one meaning and use in English. On the board, write sentences in MT containing the chosen word in English. With French as MT, an exercise for the English word 'right' could be:

1 Je le ferai right après ça.
  (I'll do it right after this.)
2 Tournez right aux prochains feux rouges.
  (Turn right at the next lights.)
3 Right, on commence.
  (Right, let's get started.)
4 C'est right au milieu du livre.
  (It's right in the middle of the book.)
5 Vous n'habitez pas ici, right?
  (You don't live here, right?)
6 C'est exactement right.
  (That's exactly right.)

**1** Ask the students to translate the English words into MT, working individually.

**2** Tell the students to check their translations in pairs and finally check with the whole class.

**3** Discuss the different use of the translated words.

## Variation

Choose a word in English that has more than one meaning. Write sentences in English with the chosen word in MT. The following exercise could be used for 'leave' / 'left':

1 I (MT word) the house early this morning.
2 He came into the room, gave me the papers and (MT word) without saying a word to anybody.
3 I (MT word) my keys at home and now I can't get back in.
4 Politically he says he's on the (MT word), but he's actually quite conservative.
5 You always (MT word) the lights on. Do you have shares in the electric company, or what?

Other suitable English words are: 'back', 'spend' and 'take'.

**Acknowledgement:** We learnt this from Tim Hahn.

# Using a Mother Tongue Spell Check

| Teacher | zero knowledge of students' MT |
|---|---|
| Class | monolingual / multilingual classes (languages with Latin script – see Variation below) |
| Level | elementary to advanced |
| Purpose | to stimulate students' linguistic intelligence |

## Preparation

For homework, ask the students to key in a page of the coursebook you are using on their computers with their MT spell check working.

Explain that many of the words in the English text will be underlined as being incorrect, but that some won't because they are also words or parts of words in the MT.

Ask the students to come to the next class with all the words that are 'OK in both languages' ringed on their print-outs. Ask them to check the English meanings of any of the ringed words that they are not sure about.

A French spell check will not underline many English words:

Pour me a whisky, <u>please, it's the</u> weekend.
('pour' = for, 'me' = to me, 'a' = at / to, 'whisky' and 'weekend' are English loan words.)

An Italian spell check will leave these words un-underlined in this text.

OK, fine, <u>just</u> come <u>here and pay my</u> fare.
('OK' is a loan word from English, 'fine' = end, 'come' = how, 'fare' = to do)

**1** Group the students in fours. In multilingual classes, ensure each group shares the same MT and get them to share and explain the meanings of the words that are 'OK in both languages'.

## Variation

Dictate an English text to your students and ask them to underline all the words that also occur visually and or auditorily in their MT. In this case, it would work across scripts auditorily.

# You Scratch My Back

| | |
|---|---|
| **Teacher** | zero knowledge of students' MT |
| **Class** | monolingual / multilingual (at least 2 students per language) |
| **Level** | beginner to lower intermediate |
| **Purpose** | to revise recently-learned vocabulary kinaesthetically |

In some cultures you can only do this exercise by putting females with females and males with males. In other cultures, touching in this way is simply not acceptable. Instead of writing on each other's backs, ask the students to finger-write on the desk / table in front of them.

## Preparation
On the board, write a list of words from recent lessons that you want your students to revise.

**1** Put the students into pairs (A and B). In multilingual classes, put them into monolingual pairs. They briefly rub each other's backs.

**2** Ask student A to finger-write one of the words in MT on student B's back. This should be done in large capital letters.

**3** Once student B has understood the MT word, they write the English translation on student A's back without speaking.

    In this way they work their way through the list of words to be revised.

## Variation
Do the same exercise with synonyms, antonyms and phrasal verbs / Latinate verbs, for example: 'put off' – 'postpone'.

# Group Vocabulary Revision

| | |
|---|---|
| **Teacher** | full knowledge of students' MT |
| **Class** | monolingual |
| **Level** | elementary to upper intermediate |
| **Purpose** | to revise vocabulary |
| **Materials** | slips of paper |

**1** Put the students into pairs. Give each student a slip of paper.

**2** Give them a lexical area you want them to work on, for example: the weather.

**3** Ask the students to think of a phrase or word in that area. For example:

    It's only spitting.

**4** Tell them to write the phrase in English on one slip of paper and in MT on another slip of paper.

**5** Take in the slips of paper and check them.

**6** Shuffle them and redistribute them round the class. Tell the students to remember what is on their slip and then to put it in a pocket or bag.

**7** Let students walk around saying their word(s) and looking for the student who has the equivalent in the other language. When they find their partner, they check it out with you.

**8** At class level, tell the students who have the MT words to read them and get the rest of the class to say the English word.

## Variation
The same technique can be used work on short conversational phrases / fillers / chunks. For example:

    What's the matter?
    As a matter of fact, ...
    You must be joking!
    I don't give a toss.
    He's such a wimp.
    I haven't a clue.
    Why doesn't that surprise me?
    It's up to you.
    You're winding me up!

# Mouthing

| Teacher | working knowledge of students' MT |
|---|---|
| Class | monolingual / multilingual groups (at least 2 students per language – see Variation below) |
| Level | beginner to lower intermediate |
| Purpose | to give students the opportunity to experience visually the words they're revising |

## Preparation
Write a list of words in a lexical area you want to consolidate with your students.

**1** Tell the students the lexical area you have chosen, for example: colours. Tell them you are going to mouth the words in MT and they have to write down the words in English.

**2** Mouth the words (i.e., don't sound them), making sure that everyone in the room can see your face. This may mean doing it three times facing a different part of the room each time.

**3** The students write down the words in English.

**4** Ask the students to go through their list and mouth back the words to you in English.

## Variation
For multilingual classes, this activity can be done in pairs. Put students into monolingual pairs. Tell them to each write their own list of MT words in a lexical area of their choice (the pairs don't have to have the same area). Tell them to take it in turns to mouth their words to each other. The partner mouths back the word in English.

# Cram as Much In as You Can

| Teacher | zero knowledge of students' MT |
|---|---|
| Class | monolingual / multilingual classes (at least 2 students per language) |
| Level | beginner to advanced |
| Purpose | to give students the chance to feel and visualise the words they're revising |
| Materials | small pieces of paper |

## Preparation
Choose a set of twenty words you want the class to revise. Write them on the board.

**1** Give out some very small squares or rectangles of paper (postage stamp size). Each student should be given two bits of paper.

**2** Ask the students to work individually and copy the list of words onto one of the bits of paper.

**3** Tell them to write all the MT translations of these words onto the other bit of paper.

**4** Ask the class to comment on how it felt to write in tiny script and whether on the whole the MT words are longer or shorter than their English equivalents.

**Acknowledgement:** We learnt the idea of cramming as many words as possible onto a small scrap of paper from Anna Curto Naffissi, who came on a Pilgrims course in June 2000.

# Chanting Vocabulary

| | |
|---|---|
| **Teacher** | zero knowledge of students' MT |
| **Class** | monolingual / multilingual classes (at least 2 students per language) |
| **Level** | beginner to lower intermediate |
| **Purpose** | to help students to fix the sounds of words in their heads |
| **Materials** | copies of list of words |

## Preparation

Make a list of twenty words you want your students to commit to memory. Make copies of the list, one for each student.

**1** Put the students into pairs. In multilingual classes, put them into monolingual pairs. Give them copies of the list you have prepared.

**2** Explain that this is a repetition exercise. The students can change from MT to English and vice versa at any time.

**3** Demonstrate the activity with one student, standing up and chanting rhythmically. With a Portuguese student, it could go like this:

| **You:** | (choosing first word from list) | butterfly |
|---|---|---|
| **Student:** | | borboleta |
| **You:** | | butterfly |
| **Student:** | | borboleta |
| **You:** | | borboleta |
| **Student:** | | butterfly |
| **You:** | | borboleta |

In demonstrating, the rhythmic part is essential. Either partner can suddenly reverse the chant and change language as the teacher does in line 5 above.

**4** Ask the pairs to stand up and chant their way through the twenty words.

**Acknowledgement:** We learnt this as part of a warm-up activity in a part-singing choir.

# Lexical Memory Aid

| | |
|---|---|
| **Teacher** | working knowledge of students' MT |
| **Class** | monolingual |
| **Level** | beginner to advanced |
| **Purpose** | to help vocabulary to stick in the mind |

## Preparation

Make a list of fifteen to thirty words you want the students to memorise along with the MT translations. Write the list on the board.

**1** Ask the students to come up with memory aids / associations / word plays in their MT to 'fix' the meaning of the English words.

A group of English students learning Kishwahili came up with the following:

| **Kurudi** (to return): | Rudy's coming home. |
|---|---|
| **Kusikia** (to hear): | He's got a sick ear. |
| **Nyoka** (snake): | ... like the wire on a Nokia phone. |

**2** Put the students into groups of four and ask them to work on associations to try to fix the words.

**3** Choose some of the best memory aids and write them up on the board.

**Acknowledgement:** The idea of bilingual mnemonic aids is one championed by Paola Hanna from Belgium. The Kishwahili examples above come from her students' work.

# True Multiple Choice

| Teacher | full knowledge of students' MT |
|---|---|
| Class | monolingual |
| Level | beginner to elementary |
| Purpose | to help students feel ownership of words they need to learn |
| Materials | sheets of paper |

## Preparation
Choose words or phrases in English that you want to consolidate. Write them on the board.

**1** Put the students into groups of four and assign one word to each group.

**2** Ask the groups to write four descriptions of their word or phrase in MT. For example:

### Competition
(The following would be written in MT.)
1 it has four syllables
2 a term often used in marketing
3 it's a noun
4 it needs to be balanced with cooperation

**3** Tell each member of the group to read out one of the statements to the rest of the class who write it down.

**4** Tell the groups to work together to decide what the word is. The first group to work it out writes it on the board.

**5** Continue like this until all the groups have read their statements.

## Variation
Groups could write three true statements and one false one about the word. The other groups then have to identify both the word and the false statement.

**NOTE:** Writing four descriptions of a word really helps the word to become lodged in the students' minds. Using MT helps them to explore the word from every possible point of view: sound, meaning, grammar, spelling, collocation, etc.

# Listening Out for Two Languages

| Teacher | zero knowledge of students' MT |
|---|---|
| Class | monolingual |
| Level | beginner to lower intermediate |
| Purpose | to help students remember words by rehearsing them in English and MT |

## Preparation
Make a bilingual list of fifteen to twenty words you want your students to revise.

**1** Get the students to move all the furniture against the walls or take them to an empty space.

**2** Ask the students to line up in two parallel rows facing you, and at an equal distance from each side wall.

```
           T
  S            S
  S            S
  S            S
```

**3** Explain that you are going to be revising vocabulary and will read out a bilingual list. Tell one row of students they are the MT Team. Tell the other row they are the English Team.

**4** Explain that you will shout out a word **either** in MT **or** in English.

- If the word is in MT, the MT Team should rush to touch the wall on their side as fast they can while the English team should try to touch them before they get to the wall.

- If an English Team member touches someone in the other team before they touch their wall, the touched person joins the English Team.

- If the word is shouted out in English, the English Team rushes to their wall and the MT Team tries to tag them before they get there.

- The aim of the game is to end up with the most people in your team.

**5** Shout out the words. Prepare to shout out the word with some neutral sound like this:
eeeeer **WATER**   or   eeeeer **NERO** (Greek)

**6** After the game, get the students that are now in the MT Team to list the MT words on the board. Tell the students that are now in the English Team to write the English translations next to them.

# Working with Loan Words

| | |
|---|---|
| **Teacher** | working knowledge of students' MT |
| **Class** | monolingual |
| **Level** | lower intermediate to advanced |
| **Purpose** | to make students aware of the English borrowings from their MT and vice versa |

## Preparation

Prepare two lists of words: words that the students' MT has borrowed from English and words that English has borrowed from their MT. For the first list, write the English words on the board with the MT words, in jumbled order, in a second column. For example:

| Words that Japanese has borrowed from English | | Key |
|---|---|---|
| 1  ball | a)  konpyuta | 1  c) |
| 2  milk | b)  miruku | 2  b) |
| 3  computer | c)  bohru | 3  a) |
| 4  television | d)  biru | 4  e) |
| 5  building | e)  terebi | 5  d) |
| 6  steering wheel | f)  super | 6  g) |
| 7  supermarket | g)  handle | 7  f) |
| 8  contact | h)  posuto | 8  i) |
| 9  leader | i)  kontakuto | 9  j) |
| 10  post | j)  lihda | 10  h) |

**1** Go through the pronunciation of the MT words and ask the students to work on the list and match up the words in the two parallel columns.

**2** Get them to chorus-read the matched words, whispering the MT words and singing the English ones.

**3** Tell the students to pick out the words where the MT version has a different meaning from the original English word.

**4** Give them your second list of words that English has borrowed from their MT.

| Words that English has borrowed from Japanese | | | |
|---|---|---|---|
| aikido | haiku | noh | sushi |
| geisha | tatami | futon | banzai |
| bonsai | kimono | samurai | origami |
| mikado | ikebana | shogun | harakiri |

**5** Ask the students to work individually on this list. Tell them to organise the words into categories and give each category a heading.

**6** Get some students to read their categories to the class and explain why they have categorised the words in this way.

**Acknowledgement:** The idea for this activity came from an article by Yamauchi Kazuaki and Stephen Lambacher in *The Language Teacher*, August 2000: 'Using English Loan Words to Teach English Pronunciation to Japanese'.

## Two-language Dictation

| | |
|---|---|
| **Teacher** | working knowledge of students' MT |
| **Class** | monolingual |
| **Level** | beginner to elementary |
| **Purpose** | to help beginners accurately guess new words in English |

### Preparation

Choose a very predictable type of text, for example, a newspaper story, in the students' MT and translate key words into English. Choose words that get repeated in the text and words that are reasonably easy to guess from the context. Make sure that you can read and dictate this mixed text fluently. (Producing the phonology of the two languages can be hard, at first.)

This is how the text could be if English were the MT and the language being taught were Modern Greek:

---

**ATTACKED WITH A RAZOR**

A youth of 18 **chronia**, who lives in Liverpool, was attacked with a razor **chthes** at around midnight in Bootle. The **travmatismenos** man, who was unable to give the **onoma** of the road, told police that he had been accosted by an **omada** of youths who tried to assault him.

One of them slashed his hand - he later received treatment in Bootle **nosokomio**.

(The words are: years, yesterday, injured, name, gang, hospital.)

---

**1** Dictate the two-language text you have prepared.

**2** Put the students into groups of three to check that they have understood the key words (i.e., those you have put in English).

**3** Ask one student to put the English words on the board in large coloured letters, with their MT translations in small black or white letters.

**4** Tell the class to get ready to draw. Dictate the English words from the passage and tell the students to make a quick drawing for each word.

**5** In a lesson a week later, dictate the same passage with double the number of words in English. You can repeat this several times, increasing the number of English words.

## Bilingual Word Association

| | |
|---|---|
| **Teacher** | working knowledge of students' MT |
| **Class** | monolingual |
| **Level** | lower intermediate to advanced |
| **Purpose** | to use MT to enrich students' vocabulary |
| **Materials** | sheets of paper |

**1** Ask someone in the class to give you a word in MT. Write it up on the board. With a student volunteer, go through a series of steps to demonstrate the activity to the class. In a class of German students, it might go like this:

| | |
|---|---|
| Original word: | **Lastwagen** |
| Student writes the English translation: | **lorry** |
| You write a free association with the word: | **sorry** |
| Student writes the MT translation: | **entschuldigen** |
| You write an MT free association: | **als Kind** |
| Student writes an English translation: | **when I was a child** |

**2** Put the students into pairs (A and B). Tell them to go through the steps that you have just demonstrated. However, they should do it in parallel, writing on separate sheets of paper, like this:

| **Student A** | | **Student B** |
|---|---|---|
| Wein | | Österreich |
| Austria | swap papers | wine |
| bottle | swap papers back | music |
| Musik | swap papers back | Flasche |

**3** Ask all the student As to start with a word you give them and all the student Bs to start with another word you give them. Tell them to do ten to fifteen exchanges.

**4** Put the pairs into groups of six. Each pair should read out what they have written, with each student reading their own bits. Tell them to read slowly.

# 3
# Skills – Input

The skills activities have been divided into 'Input' – reading and listening and 'Output' – speaking and writing. There is necessarily an overlap.

Many of the activities focus on a lead-in to a skills activity, in order to help the students to produce a more meaningful outcome. The idea is that students are encouraged to prepare themselves in their mother tongue before transferring to English. This allows them to focus on the **content** before they have to think about the **form**.

Using mother tongue enables students to tackle texts that are more difficult than their level suggests, which means that the content can be more engaging and the process more rewarding.

# Cooperative Reading Comprehension

| | |
|---|---|
| **Teacher** | full knowledge of students' MI |
| **Class** | monolingual |
| **Level** | elementary to advanced |
| **Purpose** | to use MT to enable lower level students to understand a higher level text |
| **Materials** | copies of Sheet A and Sheet B (see Preparation below) |

**NOTE:** To have half the text in MT means that the task is less daunting for the students. The English text is often difficult enough already. The point of the questions is to help students understand the text better. At this level, the language in the question should help comprehension and not offer an additional comprehension task.

This is an information-gap activity that encourages student cooperation and peer teaching.

## Preparation

Choose a text in English. It should be accompanied by comprehension questions. Translate the text and the questions into MT.

Prepare two copies of the text so that one copy contains the first half of the text in MT and the second in English (Sheet A). The other copy should be the reverse with the first half in English and the second in MT (Sheet B).

Add the comprehension questions so that they are in the opposite language to the text. See below.

| **Sheet A** | **Sheet B** |
|---|---|
| • first half of text in MT | • first half of text in English |
| • questions in English | • questions in MT |
| • space for student to answer in MT | • space for student to answer in English |
| • second half of text in English | • second half of text in MT |
| • questions in MT | • questions in English |
| • space for student to answer in English | • space for student to answer in MT |

**1** Give half the class copies of Sheet A and the other half copies of Sheet B.

**2** Ask the students to read their texts and write the answers to the questions. Tell them to write their answers in the **opposite** language to the question.

**3** Put students into pairs with the same sheets to check their answers.

**4** Pair off Sheet A and Sheet B students. Tell them to read each other's texts and then check and compare their answers.

# Student Dictates Story to Teacher

| Teacher | working knowledge of students' MT |
|---|---|
| Class | monolingual |
| Level | beginner to elementary |
| Purpose | to use MT to enable lower level students to understand a higher level text |

## Preparation
Ask one of the students to come to the next class ready to tell a personal story in as few words as possible in their MT.

**1** Ask the student to dictate their story slowly, while you write it up in English on the board. Add the MT version of every fourth or fifth word. Write this below the word and in much smaller letters.

**2** Stand back and allow the students to ask you any questions they want about the text on the board. They could be about meaning, grammar, pronunciation, or whatever they want.

**3** Ask the students to copy their classmate's text from the board.

**NOTE:** This activity is well worth doing regularly with a beginner class. It can be helpful if they have a special notebook for their classmate's stories.

**Acknowledgement:** This technique follows the common sense approach of Charles Curran's Community Language Learning, which holds that the most relevant and memorable text will come from the students.

# What Do You Mean?

| Teacher | working knowledge of students' MT |
|---|---|
| Class | monolingual |
| Level | elementary |
| Purpose | to practice intonation features |

**1** Put on the board a number of utterances in MT. For example:

Vamos   Vaya   Si   Que   No

**2** Ask the students to say the utterances, expressing as many different emotions as possible. Put them into small groups and give them some time to experiment with the differences.

**3** Ask them how many possibilities they found. If they have found just a couple, you may give them a hand by giving instructions similar to the following: 'Faster!', 'Like you're angry.'

**4** Ask the students to make a short list of similar utterances in English.

**5** Give them about five minutes to practise saying them with different emotions.

**6** Invite volunteers to say their words aloud while the rest of the group guesses what emotion they are expressing.

**NOTE:** This is one way of helping students to overcome a flat or heavily-accented pronunciation and intonation.

**Acknowledgement:** We learnt this activity from Tim Hahn.

# Teacherless Task

| Teacher | full knowledge of students' MT |
| --- | --- |
| Class | monolingual |
| Level | elementary |
| Purpose | to give elementary students the satisfaction of dealing with an intermediate level text |
| Materials | copies of English and MT versions of text, copies of same texts cut into strips (see Preparation below) |

## Preparation

Translate the text below into MT.

---

**The Barbers**

A philosopher went to visit a small town. The town was in a very big desert.

He needed a haircut. He asked if there were any barbers in town.

People told him there were two barbers in town.

People said, 'The first barber is very smart. His shop is very clean. His hair is well-cut.'

People said, 'The second barber is dirty. His shop is a mess, His hair is badly-cut.'

Both barbers worked alone. They did not have assistants.

The philosopher thought for thirty seconds. Then he went to one of the barber's shops.

**Problem:** Which barber shop did he go to? Why?

**Solution:** The clean barber with the well-cut hair could only have had his hair cut by the other one, since neither had assistants and since the town was isolated.

---

Photocopy the English and the MT version so that there is one copy for each student for use at the end of the activity.

Photocopy the English and MT version so that there is one copy for every ten students. Cut these copies up into sentence strips so that you have a cut up version of the text in both MT and English for each group of ten students (one slip per student).

This may be time-consuming, but you can use the material again and again.

**1** Group the students in tens. If your class number is wrong for this, group them in eights or nines, which will then mean that some students have two slips of paper. Alternatively, if you have a group of eleven, two students have to share a slip of paper. If possible, they should sit in closed circles.

**2** To each group of ten, give out a copy of the story in MT: one slip of paper for each student. Give out the slips **in random order**. Tell them the game rules below in MT and write them up on the board.

- Your task is to sequence the story and solve the problem.
- You may **not** write anything.
- You may read your own slip of paper out loud.
- You may **not** read anybody else's slip of paper.

**3** Ask the students to start the activity, ensuring that all the groups are working simultaneously. Allow three to five minutes for them to start sequencing in MT.

**4** Now ask the students to place all their MT sentences on the floor in the centre of their circle, face down. This includes the slips they haven't yet sequenced.

**6** Give out the English sentences in random order. Ask each student to check that they understand what is on their slip of paper. Circulate, helping the students with problems.

**7** Ask the whole group to focus on one group of ten and ask the students in that group to read their slips out. Help them with their pronunciation.

**8** Tell the students to work in their groups again. Ask them to try to sequence the story, but this time using the English text.

If a group gets lost / stuck, invite them to place their English slips on the floor and to pick up the MT ones. Let them work in MT for two to three minutes and then tell them to go back to the English slips.

**8** Tell the students to hide their MT slips. You read out the complete MT version for them to check the order of their English slips.

**9** Give out the complete story in MT and in English to each student. Collect in the slips for future use.

**10** Allow time for language questions on the parallel texts.

**NOTE:** For more stories see Appendix (page 95) and *More Grammar Games* (Davis et al., Cambridge, 1995), pages 169-172.

# Start in Mother Tongue and Finish in English

| | |
|---|---|
| **Teacher** | full knowledge of students' MT |
| **Class** | monolingual |
| **Level** | elementary |
| **Purpose** | to use MT to enable lower-level students to understand a higher level text |

## Preparation

Prepare to tell a story that the students probably do not know. Practise telling the story in English and MT.

**1** Explain to the students that you're going to tell the first half in MT and the second half in English.

**2** Put the students into groups of three to share what they understood of the second half.

**3** Tell the whole story again, but this time the first half in English and the second half in MT.

**4** Put the students into pairs and ask them to write down words or phrases from the story that they want to remember in English. Suggest that each pair bring six to eight phrases back to mind.

**5** Ask the pairs to shout out their phrases and write them up on the board. Check that everybody understands them.

**6** Ask the students to work in pairs again and retell the story in a mixture of MT and English.

**Acknowledgement:** This idea was suggested by Peter Grundy at a Matsda workshop.

# Bilingual Pre-teaching of Vocabulary

| | |
|---|---|
| **Teacher** | working knowledge of students' MT |
| **Class** | monolingual |
| **Level** | beginner to elementary |
| **Purpose** | to help students with the huge vocabulary load at beginner level |
| **Materials** | copies of text (see Preparation below), |

## Preparation

Choose a short text. Write some sentences that define the meaning of words in the text.

The example below shows how this would be done with a modern Greek text for students whose MT is English.

---

**Defining sentences**

The woman who gave birth to me is my **mitera**.
The word 'my' in Greek is **mu** and it goes after the noun.
The word **meno** means 'I live' and **meni** means 'she lives'.
To say 'a long way from' in Greek you say **makria apo**.
The word **megali** can mean 'big', but here means 'old'.

**Text**

I mitera mu meni sto Lonthino.
I mitera mu meni makria apo to kentro tu Lonthinu.
Meni sto High Barnett, 20 chilometra apo to kentro.
I mitera mu ine poli megali, 93 chronon.

---

**1** Read out the defining sentences. Tell the students to write down only the English word, not the defining sentence.

**2** Give the students the full text.

**3** Tell the students that once they have read the English text, you are ready to answer any MT questions they have about meanings, word order, grammar, pronunciation, intonation, spelling or collocations. Don't tell them what they ought to be asking about!

## Variation

At higher levels, you can do the above activity all in English. If there are twenty words you think the students will not know in a reading passage, read definition sentences **in English**, and tell them to take down the words. Then they read the passage.

**Acknowledgement:** We learnt the technique in the Variation from an Oslo teacher called Gudrun.

# Listen and Find

| | |
|---|---|
| **Teacher** | full knowledge of students' MT |
| **Class** | monolingual |
| **Level** | elementary to upper intermediate |
| **Purpose** | to encourage students to work out the meaning of new words and phrases |
| **Materials** | copies of text (see Preparation below) |

## Preparation
Choose a text you want your students to read. This could be from the coursebook. Pick out about eight words or phrases. This could be language you predict they will not know, and / or collocations and chunks you want them to focus on. Translate these words into MT.

**1** Give the students the text. Tell them to look at the text while you call out the MT words and chunks on your list in the order in which they appear in the text. While listening to the MT words, students should underline the English equivalent in the text.

**2** Read the words again, but this time in random order. Tell the students to listen and circle the English equivalent in the text.

**3** Put the students into pairs and ask them to compare their work and recall the MT equivalents.

**4** Get the pairs to take it in turns to call out one of the MT words or chunks and ask the rest of the class to call out the English in the text.

## Variation
This could also be done with a listening text. In this case, write your MT words on the board and ask the students to raise their hands when they hear the English equivalents.

# Home-grown Reading Comprehension

| | |
|---|---|
| **Teacher** | zero knowledge of students' MT (can prepare with the help of a student interpreter) |
| **Class** | monolingual / multilingual |
| **Level** | beginner to elementary |
| **Purpose** | to get the students to provide a student-generated personal reading comprehension |
| **Materials** | copies of story (see Preparation below) |

## Preparation
Get a student from your class to tell you any story from their past that they don't mind their classmates reading. You can elicit the story in MT or English. If you don't know MT, you'll need an interpreter.

Write the story in English so that it is a linguistically challenging reading comprehension for the class.

Give a copy of the story to its owner just before class, if possible, so **they** can check through and be sure they understand the words.

Copy the story so there is one text for each student.

**1** Give copies of the text to the students. Tell them whose story the text is and leave this student to run the class for five to ten minutes.

**2** Take charge of the class again and do any vocabulary or grammar work that the text lends itself to.

**3** Get a volunteer for the next reading comprehension story and fix a time to see them.

## Variation 1
When you write up the story the student has told you, make some content mistakes, so that they will have to get the other students to correct their texts in class.

## Variation 2
When you write up the story, make some logical / semantic mistakes that an intelligent reader will want to correct. For example:

My **sister's** name is Naraporn. **He** is older than me ...

# Guess the Answers

| | |
|---|---|
| **Teacher** | zero knowledge of students' MT |
| **Class** | monolingual / multilingual classes (at least 2 students per language) |
| **Level** | lower intermediate to advanced |
| **Purpose** | to use MT to get students to predict the content of a text before they have read it |
| **Materials** | copies of text (see Preparation below) |

## Preparation

Choose a text from your coursebook or elsewhere. Write some questions about the text in English, or use the questions in the coursebook.

**1** Give the students the title of the text they are going to read.

**2** Read out the questions and ask the students to guess the answers and write them in MT. They should **not** write the questions.

**3** Put the students into pairs or small groups and get them to compare their answers. They can do this in English and / or MT. As they have had to guess the answers, there will be a rich variety of ideas.

**4** Tell the students to look at their answers again and use these to write the original questions you dictated in English, leaving a space between each one.

**5** Get the students to check their questions in pairs and finally at class level.

**6** Now give them the English text to read.

**7** Tell them to write the text-inspired answers to the questions in English.

## Variation

This technique can also be used with a listening text.

# A Matter of Preference

| | |
|---|---|
| **Teacher** | working knowledge of students' MT |
| **Class** | monolingual |
| **Level** | elementary to upper intermediate |
| **Purpose** | to foster full listening comprehension |

## Preparation

Choose two houses you know well, one of which you like and one of which you dislike, and prepare to describe each house in English to the class as neutrally as possible. Use very simple sentences.

**1** Tell the students you are going to describe two houses, one of which you like and one you don't. They need to decide which house is which. Describe both houses **neutrally**.

**2** Put the students into groups of four to discuss in MT which of the two houses they think you prefer.

**3** Now ask the students to vote. When you get the first show of hands for house No.1, get them to justify their decision in MT. Write some of the MT sentences up on the board small and the English versions large.

**4** In the same way, write up some of the justifications for thinking you prefer house No.2.

**5** Tell the students which house you actually prefer.

**6** Get them to read out the sentences you have put up on the board in English.

**7** Rub out one word in each sentence. Tell the students to read the sentences again, with the missing words.

**8** Rub out two more words from each sentence and get them to read them with the missing words in.

**9** Continue to do this with all the words. They should finally be able to 'read' the sentences with no English words left on the board.

## Variation

You can do this exercise with two of anything, providing you genuinely like one and dislike the other: men, pets, cars, politicians, dishes, films, etc.

At higher levels, you can do this exercise entirely in English and then ask a student to come to class ready to produce two neutral texts about two objects, one of which they like and one of which they don't.

# Deal with My Post

| Teacher | full knowledge of students' MT |
|---|---|
| Class | monolingual |
| Level | lower to upper intermediate |
| Purpose | to give students realistic practice of reading a text in English and summarising briefly in MT |
| Materials | selection of correspondence (see Preparation below) |

## Preparation

Collect a range of postal or e-mail communications you have received in English, including junk mail, bills, reminders, begging letters from charities, business letters, personal letters, etc. You need one item for each student in your class. If you don't get that much stuff in English, then borrow a 'postbag' from a friend in an English-speaking country.

**1** Give the students this mass of e-mails, letters, etc. and ask each one to take one document, read it through and be ready to summarise its main points to you in MT.

**2** Circulate, helping with language and culture problems.

**3** Ask each student to tell you and the class briefly, in MT, what is in the document they have read.

**NOTE:** Teenagers are sometimes asked by a relative to translate the minimal gist of a letter that has arrived from 'out there'. Such letters are often in English. The activity above prepares them for this sort of situation.

**Acknowledgement:** We found the idea in the Note above in the work of Bessie Dendrinos, Athens University, Greece.

# From Internal Text to English

| Teacher: | working knowledge of students' MT |
|---|---|
| Class | monolingual |
| Level | beginner |
| Purpose | to get students used to the sound of English / to make chunks of English sound meaningful |

## Preparation

Choose a story that your students will be familiar with: a well-known folk story, for example. Prepare to tell it, rather than read it, in English.

**1** Write the title of the tale you are going to tell on the board in English and in MT.

**2** Ask the students to work individually and write down ten to fifteen key words from the story in MT.

**3** Ask them to bring to mind a moment from the story and then draw it.

**4** Put the students into small groups and ask them to compare their drawings and words.

**5** Get the students to put their key words on the board. Tell them to write very small and in a quiet colour.

**6** With their help, write in the English translations of all the key words. Use a bright colour for this and write large.

**7** Tell the whole story to the group in English, lightly stressing the key words and pointing to them on the board. As you go through the story, replace the single key words with phrases, so that 'wolf' becomes 'big bad wolf', for example.

**8** Put the students into pairs (A and B). Ask student A to tell the first half of the story to student B. They can do this in MT using as much English as they can. Tell student B to do the same with the second part of the story.

**NOTE:** This technique is powerful in that it endows the distant, odd sounds and shapes of the foreign language with the context of a familiar text.

# Mixed Language Story-telling

| Teacher | full knowledge of students' MT |
|---|---|
| Class | monolingual |
| Level | beginner to elementary |
| Purpose | to use MT listening as preparation for English listening and comprehension |

## Preparation

This is an activity that can extend over several lessons. The main preparation, however, is done for the first lesson.

Choose a story you are happy to tell and mumble it through to yourself in MT. It is best to choose a story the students do not yet know. Note down the words and phrases you are going to put into English on a slip of paper. The words you choose should be the key nouns and verbs of the story. For a first telling, have fifteen to twenty words or phrases in English.

As you rehearse your telling, be sure to stress the English words, not the MT ones. (This is why the Greek words in the example below are in bold type.) It is **vital** that you give the students enough information about each English word for its meaning to be absolutely clear.

You can use mime, pictures, blackboard drawings, MT explanations or straight translations. Once you have launched a word or phrase in English, never use the MT version again.

This is an example of the technique used to teach Modern Greek, to English students.

> Once upon a time there was a bear, and this **arkutha** - **arkutha** means bear - well, as I was telling you this **arkutha** was walking through the **thaso** - you understand **thaso** - a place with many trees, many trees make a **thaso** ... Anyway, the **arkutha** was walking through the **thaso**, when suddenly the **arkutha** looked up and saw the wild **pulia** flying to the South. The **arkutha** thought to herself, 'When the **pulia** fly to the South then it is **ora** *(here the story-teller points to their watch)* **na kimitho**. *(Here the story-teller puts their head on one side and mimes sleeping.)* ...

## Lesson 1

**1** Tell the students the mixed language story with as much clarity and energy as you can muster.

**2** After the telling, ask them to call out any words they remember. As they say them, write them up on the board to help visually-focused students. Be kind, and honour the student who just remembers one syllable, or who remembers the tune of a phrase but not the exact sounds.

**3** Tell the story a second time, but this time pause at the English bits so they can chorus the words.

## Lesson 2

**4** Tell the story again, but this time with twice the number of words and phrases in English.

You can do this either by saying completely new items in English or by increasing the islands of English. So, if in the first lesson you had 'fox' in English, in the second telling you might expand to 'cunning old fox'.

## Lesson 3

**5** Tell the story again, this time with as many new words in English as you feel they can manage.

**6** Put the students into groups of three to retell the story bilingually, using as much English as they can.

**7** Retell the story yourself for the last time, this time all in English.

NOTE: We believe that mixed language story-telling is among the most powerful of the mixed language techniques presented in this book, because the text comes to the learner from **you**: **your** voice, **your** gestures, your way of being and all this forms part of the relationship between you and your students.

Leaving aside Anthony Burgess' *Clockwork Orange*, an English text peppered with Russian, we know of two language teaching texts that use the 'language sandwich' technique: *Dear Doosie* (Werner von Lansburgh, Fischer Verlag, 1979) and *Red Yellow Blue: a Chinese / English Story Garden for Children*, (Ji-Yuha, Fuzhou, Fujian People's Publishing House, 1998).

# Words from a Story

| Teacher | full knowledge of students' MT |
|---|---|
| Class | monolingual |
| Level | beginner |
| Purpose | to ease students' way into listening to a story |

**1** Tell a one / two minute story in MT.

**2** Write about eight key words from the story on the board in MT.

**3** Add the English translations next to each word in large, coloured letters. Practise the pronunciation.

**4** Act out each word in random order. Tell the students to call out the words in English.

**5** Put the students into pairs. Ask them to repeat this last step.

**6** Draw pictures of the words on the board for the students to label, or invite different students to do this.

**7** Read out the words in English and ask the students to make and write a verbal or pictorial association for each word. The verbal association should be in MT.

**8** Ask the students to write the English words next to each association.

**9** Get the students to share their associations.

**10** Retell the story in MT, but stop before each key word so that the students can provide the word in English.

**11** If appropriate, retell the whole story in English

**Acknowledgement:** We learnt this activity from teachers on a Creative Teacher Course at Pilgrims.

# Two-language Chinese Whispers

| Teacher | zero knowledge of students' MT |
|---|---|
| Class | monolingual |
| Level | elementary to lower intermediate |
| Purpose | to encourage students to listen and spontaneously translate |
| Materials | story written on slips of paper (see Preparation below) |

## Preparation

Choose a story, anecdote, or joke at the right level for your class and write it out into short sentences in English. There may well be material in your coursebook that would be suitable.

You will be dividing your class into groups of six. The number of sentences must correspond to the number of groups you have. Write each sentence in English on a separate slip of paper.

**1** Put students into teams of six (A, B, C, etc.).

**2** Give student A in each group one of the sentences so that each group is working on a different one. Don't hand them out in the order of the story.

**3** Tell student A to translate the sentence into MT and then whisper it to student B. Student B then translates it back into English and whispers it to student C. Student C then translates it back into MT, and so on.

**4** Tell each student to write down what they have whispered and not to show anyone.

**5** When all the groups have finished, the last student to receive the sentence in one of the groups writes the sentence on the board in both languages. Then student A of the same group writes the sentence they whispered on the board. If there is a big difference between the sentences, ask the other students in the group to write the sentence they whispered on the board so that they can see where things changed. Use the same procedure with each group.

**6** When all the original sentences are on the board, each group works on putting the sentences in the right order to produce the story. The first group to finish reads it out to the class.

# Understand the Question from the Answer

| | |
|---|---|
| **Teacher** | working knowledge of students' MT |
| **Class** | monolingual |
| **Level** | beginner to elementary |
| **Purpose** | to help beginners get the gist of eight to ten complete sentences in English that are taken from an authentic text |
| **Materials** | copies of prepared interview (see Preparation below) |

## Preparation

Choose a written interview in the students' MT and replace the MT questions with ones in English. Photocopy the adapted interview for each student.

For a class of English students learning Italian, the text might look something like this:

**Interview with a Kidnap Victim**

**Question:** Signora W, quando è stata rapita?

**Answer:** I was kidnapped on the night of July 21st, at 2.30 am.

**Question:** Per quanti giorni è stata nelle loro mani?

**Answer:** 'In their hands ...', I don't like the expression ... I was in their hands for 87 days.

**Question:** Qual è stato il momento piú drammatico?

**Answer:** The moment they seized me. I was afraid of what they might do to me.

**Question:** Cosa mangiava?

**Answer:** Potatoes and rice ... I'm afraid I put on quite a few kilos.

**1** Put the students into pairs and give each pair one copy of the interview you have prepared to each pair. Ask them to read it.

**2** Ask them to reread the interview and underline all the words and phrases in the English questions they think they understand.

**3** Put the first question on the board and ask some students to come and write the best translation they can find for it. Only help the students if they are stuck, or hypothesising wildly.

**4** Go through all the questions in a similar way.

**5** Work with one student who reads well in MT. Read out the interview so that you are asking the English questions and the student is giving the MT answers.

**6** Dramatise the interview again with you and the whole class reading the English questions chorally and the good MT reader saying the answers.

**7** Give out all the remaining interview texts so that each student has a copy.

# 4
# Skills – Output

The skills activities have been divided into 'Input' – reading and listening and 'Output' – speaking and writing. There is necessarily an overlap.

Many of the activities focus on a lead-in to a skills activity, in order to help students produce a more meaningful outcome. They are encouraged to prepare themselves in their mother tongue before transferring to English. This allows them to focus on the content before they have to think about the form.

The natural process of preparing for the less familiar by calling on the support of the familiar enables students to gain confidence and fluency in both their speaking and writing.

# A First Go at Writing

| | |
|---|---|
| **Teacher** | working knowledge of students' MT |
| **Class** | monolingual |
| **Level** | beginner to elementary |
| **Purpose** | to encourage students to write whatever they can in English, using MT as a fallback device |
| **Materials** | copies of letter (see Preparation below) |

## Preparation

Write a letter to the class in English at a language level that the students will just be able to understand. Your text should be challenging

**1** Give out a copy of your letter to each student and ask them to read it. Circulate, helping individual students with comprehension.

**2** Ask the students to write a letter in reply to yours. Tell them to write whatever they can in English and the rest in MT. Circulate, helping them with individual queries as they are writing.

An English student learning Indonesian might produce something like this:

> Dear **ibu guru** (Mrs Teacher),
>
> **Saya** (I) want to know where the **Indonesia Bahasa** (language) comes from. **Saya** guess that **satu**, **dua**, **tiga** (one, two, three) are ...

**3** Collect in all the letters. Choose one that has a lot of English in it and get the writer's permission to put it up on the board. Write up the mixed language text.

**4** Get the class' help to turn all the MT parts into English.

**5** Tell the students to copy the English text from the board.

**NOTE:** In the next lesson you may want to give the students a group reply to all their letters.

# Translating What You Wrote Me

| | |
|---|---|
| **Teacher** | working knowledge of students' MT |
| **Class** | monolingual / multilingual (at least 2 students per language) |
| **Level** | elementary to advanced |
| **Purpose** | to provide in-depth reading of another person's text supported by a translation task, leading into writing in English |
| **Materials** | sheets of paper |

**1** Put the students into pairs. In multilingual classes, put them into monolingual pairs. Tell the partners to sit away from each other.

**2** Ask each student to write a one-page letter in MT to their partner (or less at elementary level), on whatever topic they wish.

**3** Ask the pairs to exchange their letters. They should then translate the letter received into English and write a reply in English.

**4** Tell the students to sit with their partner and read the replies and compare notes on the translation.

**5** In a monolingual class, ask the students to put the phrases that were hard to translate into English up on the board. Work on these difficulties with the whole class.

**6** Invite comments on the process the students have been through.

**NOTE:** The point of writing in MT first is to allow the students, especially at low levels, to really express themselves fully.

# Code-switching in Writing

| | |
|---|---|
| **Teacher** | full knowledge of students' MT |
| **Class** | monolingual |
| **Level** | lower intermediate to advanced |
| **Purpose** | to use MT to activate writing in English |
| **Materials** | sheets of paper |

**1** Ask the students to get up and move around the room. As they are doing this, ask them to find themselves a partner – not someone who usually sits near them.

**2** Tell them to go back and sit down in their original places.

**3** Ask each student to write a one-page letter to their partner. The letter must start in English but explain that the writers can **code-switch** between English and MT as much as they wish.

**4** Tell the students to deliver their letters to their partners. The partner should then translate the letter; MT bits into English and English bits into MT.

**5** Tell the pairs to sit together and look at the original letters and the translated ones. Get the writers to explain their process and why they switched language where they did.

**6** Deal with any language problems that have come up.

**NOTE:** The positive influence of writing with less impediment in MT is likely to flow into writing in English

**Acknowledgement:** We received 'permission' to think of encouraging students to code-switch (something bilinguals are always up to) in a plenary Claire Kramsch gave at the IATEFL International Conference in 1998.

# Family History

| | |
|---|---|
| **Teacher** | zero knowledge of students' MT |
| **Class** | monolingual / multilingual |
| **Level** | lower intermediate to advanced |
| **Purpose** | to enable students to read about each other's families in English, and to include their stories in the school website / magazine |

## Preparation

This is an activity that is best spread over a couple of lessons.

For homework, ask the students to interview their parents or grandparents and make notes in MT about how things have changed over their lifetimes.

**1** Put the students into groups of three and ask them to report in English from the notes they have taken.

**2** For homework, ask the students to write up what they have been told by the older people in English.

**3** Explain that these stories are to go up on the school website or magazine, so they must be in as good English as possible. Ask the students to correct each other's texts and to call you over if they need you. This is an ideal time to focus on accuracy as the student feels a real motivation and need to get things 100% correct.

**4** Get the students to key in the texts and put the project up on the school website or magazine.

**Acknowledgement:** We met this idea in the work of Luke Prodromou and he says he learnt the idea from the A-Z School of English, Thessaloniki, Greece.

# Key Word Dialogues

| | |
|---|---|
| **Teacher** | working knowledge of students' MT |
| **Class** | monolingual |
| **Level** | beginner to elementary |
| **Purpose** | activating new vocabulary in context |

**1** Choose a situation, for example, enquiring about the cheapest times to travel by train.

**2** Put the students into pairs and ask them to identify three key words that they don't know in English that are relevant to the situation. Ask them to write these on the board in MT.

**3** As a class, get the students to try to translate all the words into English. Stand back and observe.

**4** Explain that each pair is responsible for finding an English translation for any of the words that remain untranslated. At this point, help when necessary.

**5** Tell the students to work in pairs and write a dialogue for the situation, incorporating at least five of the new words. As they do this, you can check the dialogues.

**6** This could be followed up in a number of ways depending on space, time, and the size of the class.
  - Get each pair to read out their dialogue to the class.
  - Get each pair to dictate their dialogue to the class.
  - Tell pairs to mill around, reading their dialogues to other pairs.
  - Display the dialogues on the wall and get pairs to vote for the one they like best.

**NOTE:** This technique could also be used to lead into a dialogue in the coursebook.

# You Do the Bits I Can't Do

| | |
|---|---|
| **Teacher** | full knowledge of students' MT |
| **Class** | monolingual |
| **Level** | beginner to elementary |
| **Purpose** | to use MT to let students say exactly what they want |

**1** Put the students into groups of about five.

**2** Ask each group to think of one or two sentences in MT on any topic, for example: 'what happened yesterday'.

**3** Tell them to translate as much of the sentences into English as they can, leaving gaps for the unknown words.

**4** Ask them to put their English words, with gaps for the missing words, on the board. For example:

| | | |
|---|---|---|
| Friday | work | tired |
| computer | telephone | facial |
| money | | |

**5** Ask the students to give you their complete, original sentence in MT.

**6** Translate these into English and fill in the gaps between their words on the board or reformulate the sentences into better ones. For example:

> On **Friday** I was meant to **work**. I was fed up with my **computer**, so I **telephoned** a salon to book a **facial**. It cost a lot of **money**.

**7** Tell the students to copy the completed English sentence.

**8** Tell the students to choose one of the sentences on the board and modify it by changing any words that you did not write (i.e., the words in bold). They can do this in English or MT.

> On **Monday** I was meant to **do my homework**. I was fed up with my **teacher** so I **telephoned** a **friend** to go out. We spent a lot of **money**.

**9** Translate any unknown words and get the students to write out the sentences again in English

# How Do Parents Sound in English?

| | |
|---|---|
| **Teacher** | zero knowledge of students' MT |
| **Class** | monolingual / multilingual |
| **Level** | elementary to advanced |
| **Purpose** | to translate the language of the home into English and to see how it feels |

## Preparation

Think of three or four expressions from your childhood, things that were said over and over again. Write them in English. Mario's example is:

**Mother:** Pick your feet up – shoe leather costs money.

**1** Write up a few of your home clichés on the board in MT and in English and explain who said them, when, and in what sort of voice.

**2** Put the students into groups and ask them to nominate a secretary for their group.

**3** Get the class to brainstorm some of their home clichés and ask the group secretaries to come to the board to write them up.

**4** If your class is monolingual, ask the secretary to write them up in MT and English. If it is multilingual, ask each student to try to translate their sentence into English, and only put up the English version.

**5** When they have filled the board, ask each student to say their sentences in both languages in the way the family member would have said them.

**6** Get the class reading the English versions chorally.

## Extension

**1** Put the students into groups of four. Ask them to make a list of new family utterances that have occurred to them over the past few minutes.

**2** Using this list and the one on the board, ask them to produce a short 'parent poem' in MT, in English or in a mix of the two. The quoted utterances should form the bulk of the poem.

**3** Ask the groups to stick their poems up round the walls for everyone to read.

# Seen from Many Sides

| | |
|---|---|
| **Teacher** | zero knowledge of students' MT |
| **Class** | monolingual / multilingual |
| **Level** | lower intermediate to advanced |
| **Purpose** | to notice the effects of switching languages and viewpoints |
| **Materials** | sheets of paper |

**1** Ask each student to bring to mind a disagreement, discussion or conflict they are having or have recently had with another person.

**2** Tell them to write between half a page and one page about the conflict situation in MT. Make it clear that no one else will see what they have written.

**3** Ask half a dozen students to come to the board and draw an elephant each. (This is to help the writers to quickly come out of what they have been writing.)

**4** Tell each student to take a new sheet of paper and mentally become their adversary in the conflict. Tell them to write half a page about the conflict from the adversary's point of view, but this time **in English**.

**5** Tell six students to come to the board and draw the Eiffel Tower, but upside down.

**6** Ask each student to take a fresh sheet of paper and write a headline and three paragraphs about the conflict **in MT** as if they were a reporter, seeing it from outside.

**7** Ask the students to re-read the three texts they have written and compare them. They can express this comparison as a drawing, diagram, using colours, etc., in a non-verbal way.

**8** Finally, ask the students to write three sentences about the conflict from their point of view **in English**.

**9** Allow time for a general feedback session and ask what effect changing languages had on people.

**NOTE:** In this activity students write only for themselves. In doing this they are making a very strong, positive statement about the status of English in their minds and hearts. This activity will best suit students with strong intra-personal needs and intelligence.

# Bilingual Letters Round the Class

| Teacher | working knowledge of students' MT |
|---|---|
| Class | monolingual |
| Level | beginner to lower intermediate |
| Purpose | to give the students the opportunity to write as much of a text as they can in English |
| Materials | sheets of paper |

**1** Tell the students they are going to spend thirty minutes writing letters to each other across the class about whatever topics they want. Ask them to write as much as they can in English and the rest in their MT. If they are Spanish speakers, they might produce bits of text like this:

> Dear Enrique,
>
> I am muy happy de escribir you today.

**2** As soon as a student finishes a letter, they should deliver it to its addressee. As soon as they receive a letter, they should answer it.

**3** Tell the students that they can ask you for as much help as they want, so more of their text can be in English than in MT. Circulate, helping with their questions.

**4** After twenty minutes of this free, bilingual writing, ask them to finish off their correspondences. Give them three to four minutes to do this.

**5** Ask if any pair (writer and recipient) is willing to dictate their bilingual letter to you on the board.

**6** Write it up entirely in English.

**7** Do the same with a second letter.

# Letter Beginnings and Endings

| Teacher | working knowledge of students' MT |
|---|---|
| Class | monolingual |
| Level | lower intermediate to advanced |
| Purpose | to teach the register of formulaic beginnings and endings to letters |

## Preparation
Ask the students to bring in about five letters they or their family have received to the next class. They should all be in MT. If possible, they should be a mixture of personal and business-type letters.

**1** Tell the students to copy out the beginnings and endings of their letters in MT.

**2** Write some typical beginnings and endings for letters in English on the board. For example:

| Beginnings | Endings |
|---|---|
| Dear | With love from |
| My Dear | Lots of love |
| Dearest | Yours sincerely, |
| Hi | Yours faithfully |
| | Yours truly |
| | Yours |
| | As ever |
| | Best wishes |

**3** Tell the students to find the nearest English equivalent to their MT beginnings and endings.

**4** Put the students into pairs (A and B). Tell them to exchange their MT letters.

**5** Ask student A to read out their English equivalents of the beginnings and endings and student B to identify the matching MT version.

**6** Tell them to swap roles and do it the other way round.

# Minimal Dialogues

| | |
|---|---|
| **Teacher** | zero knowledge of students' MT |
| **Class** | monolingual / multilingual |
| **Level** | beginner |
| **Purpose** | to show the students how good they are at exploring English |
| **Materials** | CD / cassette player, coloured pens, OHP / A3 sheet of paper (see Preparation below), dictionaries (optional) |

## Preparation

Choose a short dialogue from the coursebook or some other source. If the dialogue does not come from the coursebook, you will also need to make a recording of it.

Prepare an OHP transparency of the dialogue or write it out on a sheet of A3 paper.

Pick out between seven and ten key words / phrases from the dialogue and write them on the board in large, coloured letters. Do this in random order all over the board. Write the translation of each word underneath it in small black letters (you will need help if you do not know the students' MT).

**1** Put the students into pairs and ask them to make up a dialogue using these words and these words **only**.

**2** Ask some pairs round the class to read out their dialogues.

**3** Play the recording of the dialogue twice.

**4** Show them the dialogue on the OHP or A3 sheet of paper.

**5** Ask them to look at the full text and tell them you will answer any questions they have. Give full answers to their questions but resist the temptation of answering questions they have not asked.

**Acknowledgement:** We learnt this technique from Dave Allen, a teacher at NILE, Norwich. He remembers learning it from a colleague who worked in the Persian-Arab Gulf. Techniques migrate.

# Making Fun of English Sounds

| | |
|---|---|
| **Teacher** | zero knowledge of students' MT |
| **Class** | monolingual |
| **Level** | beginner to lower intermediate |
| **Purpose** | to internalise English phonology while making fun of English sounds |
| **Materials** | English and MT versions of reading text (see Preparation below) |

## Preparation

Translate, or ask someone else to translate, a text into the students' MT. See examples below. Make copies of the English and the MT versions.

> 1   English sounds horrible.
>     The Americans sound terrible.
>     Some are lazy – they don't speak (MT).
>     Some try.
>     They can't speak it well.
>     They make me laugh.
>     They are so stupid.
>     They are so ugly.
>     Will pigs ever fly?
>
> 2   I'm embarrassed about my English.
>     I know I make a lot of mistakes.
>     I think people are laughing at me.
>     I don't feel me in English.
>     But I really need to learn it.
>     It's a hard job.

**1** Give out the MT text and ask the students to read it and imagine how a typical English speaker who spoke their MT badly would pronounce these words. Ask the students to rehearse reading it with a funny English / American accent. Tell them to practise quietly.

**2** Ask for volunteers to demonstrate.

**3** Give out the English version of the text. Ask the students to rehearse reading this with the same 'funny' English accent.

**4** Get some volunteers to try to read out loud in front of the class.

# Mixed-ability Discussions

| | |
|---|---|
| **Teacher** | full knowledge of students' MT |
| **Class** | monolingual |
| **Level** | lower intermediate to advanced (see diagram) |
| **Purpose** | to give all students in a multi-level class the opportunity to participate in a discussion |
| **Materials** | sheets of paper |

**1** Put students into groups of five.

**2** Tell the groups to choose a topic that they want to discuss in English. This may be a general discussion, or a negotiation. For example: arranging to send a group of students to an English speaking institution.

**3** Organise the students as follows:

Student A speaks only MT. (lower level)
Student B speaks only English. (middle level)
Student C speaks both, so is the interpreter. (higher level)
Students D and E are scribes and write only in English.
Student D writes the interpreter's English version of what Student A says.
Student E writes down everything said by Student B.

**4** Give a time limit for the discussion. It's hard work for the scribes so ten minutes is probably about right.

**5** At the end of the activity, tell the groups to go through the language written by their scribes. They should reformulate and edit anything they feel needs changing. Tell them to hand you their corrected version.

**6** Take the scribes' work home so you can go through the language, reformulating and editing as you think is useful.

**NOTE:** This is a useful activity for ESP and Business English.

# Three-phase Discussions

| | |
|---|---|
| **Teacher** | zero knowledge of students' MT |
| **Class** | monolingual / multilingual classes (at least 3 students per language) |
| **Level** | lower intermediate to advanced |
| **Purpose** | to encourage students to listen to each other and to relay other people's ideas accurately |

**1** Set up a discussion topic that will interest your class. You could do this by offering a choice and getting the class to vote on their favourite. Alternatively, ask students to write suggestions on the board and then have a vote.

**2** Put students into groups of three to six. In multilingual classes, put them into monolingual groups.

**3** Tell each group to appoint a scribe to make notes in MT on the main points covered. The discussion can last up to ten minutes. It can be in MT or in English.

**4** Ask the scribes to read out the points that were made one at a time to their groups. Tell the group to translate the main points of the discussion into English.

**5** Rearrange the groups so that there is at least one student from each original group in the new groups. Starting with the smallest group, give each person in the group a number, for example, one to four. Then regroup the class into groups of number ones, twos, threes and fours. In multilingual classes, regroup the students into multilingual groups of about four.

**6** Ask each student to report on the discussion they have just had with their previous group and do this in English.

**NOTE:** This process enables students to think of the content before embarking on a complicated discussion in English. They also have the responsibility of relaying what they and their group discussed to other students, thereby ensuring that everyone takes part.

# Respectful Dialogues

| | |
|---|---|
| **Teacher** | full knowledge of students' MT |
| **Class** | monolingual / multilingual classes (at least 3 students per language) |
| **Level** | lower intermediate to advanced |
| **Purpose** | to help people to listen to each other and to learn to interpret quickly from MT to English and vice versa |

**1** Put students into groups of three (A, B and C) and explain that the groups are going to create a free dialogue. Student A will speak in English, student B in MT and student C will be a scribe. Students A and B have to translate what their partner has just said before they answer.

**2** To make the activity clear to the students, demonstrate it with one of them. Get a volunteer and find a topic you disagree with this person on. For example, if the MT is Spanish and the topic is 'Being on Time', the conversation might go like this:

> **Teacher:** I think that people should always be on time.
> **Student:** (Translation) Creo que todos debemos siempre llegar a tiempo.
> (Response) Hay otras cosas mucho más importantes que la puntualidad.
> **Teacher:** (Translation) There are other things that are a great deal more important than being punctual.
> (Response) You say that because you're often late!
> **Student:** (Translation) ¡Tu dices esto porque a menudo llegas tarde!
> (Response) No es justo, no llego casi nunca tarde!
> **Teacher:** (Translation) That's not fair, I hardly ever arrive late ...

**3** In the groups, ask the students A and B to face each other and student C to stand to one side. Student C should write down as much as they can of the bilingual dialogue A and B are going to have.

**4** Ask students A and B in each group to pick a topic they disagree about and start their bilingual dialogue, with C taking notes.

**5** Allow three minutes for the dialogue. Stop the students and ask student C to feedback to A and B what they said and how well they interpreted. Allow time for discussion.

**6** Ask them to repeat the exercise, but with a change of roles, so student C has a chance to participate in the dialogue.

**7** Ask the students to change roles again, so that everybody has worked as student C.

**8** Allow time for feedback on how the students felt during the activity.

**NOTE:** This is a counselling exercise in which a person has to give proof of having listened to the other before coming in with a response. Interpreting between the two languages makes it hard for any one to indulge in normal conversational egoism.

# Student-generated Mutual Dictation

| | |
|---|---|
| **Teacher** | working knowledge of students' MT |
| **Class** | monolingual |
| **Level** | lower intermediate to advanced |
| **Purpose** | to encourage thinking in 2 languages to promote cooperative learning in a mixed-ability class |
| **Materials** | sheets of paper |

**1** Put students into pairs so that a stronger student (A) is working with a weaker student (B).

**2** Let them choose a topic or give them a topic to talk about. For example:

    learning English
    the ideal teacher
    the perfect birthday
    the Internet
    public transport

**3** Tell the students that they going to have a conversation where student A speaks in English and student B speaks in MT. They should write down everything their partner says, leaving a space between each utterance, so that they are writing out a one-sided dialogue.

**4** Get student A to start the conversation by saying a short sentence in English. Student B should write down this sentence.

**5** Student B then responds in MT and student A writes down this sentence.

**6** Tell them to continue like this until they have both said about four sentences. At this point, student A will have four sentences written in MT with a space for the first line and in between each written sentence. Student B will have four sentences written in English with a space after the first line and between each sentence.

It could look something like this:

| **Student A's sheet** |
|---|
| _____ |
| Ça va, mais il y a trop à apprendre. |
| _____ |
| Apprendre les mots, ça va. C'est la grammaire que je déteste. |
| _____ |
| Moi aussi. Ils parlent si vite. |
| _____ |
| Évidemment. Mais le français est beaucoup plus facile! |

| **Student B's sheet** |
|---|
| Do you like English? |
| _____ |
| Yes, all the words, and the grammar. |
| _____ |
| My problem is understanding the cassette. |
| _____ |
| But we speak fast in French. |

**7** Tell the students to translate their partner's sentences that they have taken down. Student A will translate from MT to English, student B will translate from English to MT.

**8** Tell the pairs to do a mutual dictation. They should dictate their translated sentences to each other and write them in the spaces of their one-sided dictations.

**9** Get them to look at their completed dictations; student A's in MT and student B's in English, and make any necessary adjustments.

**10** Tell them to read out the English text together.

# How I'm Feeling

| Teacher | full knowledge of student's MT |
|---|---|
| Class | monolingual |
| Level | beginner to lower intermediate |
| Purpose | to use MT to help students express their feelings in English |
| Materials | different coloured marker pens / chalk |

**1** Ask the students to give you a single sentence in MT that expresses how they feel right at this moment. In large classes, get students to write in pairs or small groups. Write up each sentence in English on the board in large letters. Write each sentence in a different colour, with the MT version below it in small letters.

**2** Get the class to chorus the English sentences on the board so they get the feeling of each sentence.

**3** Ask the students to get up and move around the room, saying the sentence they like best in English to other people as they pass them.

**4** Prepare a copy of what was on the board. Put all the English sentences in large typeface with MT underneath in smaller letters. Give this out to the students in the next lesson.

## Variation

Ask the student to express their beginning-of-class mood in terms of the weather. For example:

I feel cloudy today.
There is thunder and lightening around.
Rain and sunny spells.
The temperature has fallen to minus 20.

This is a marvellous way to teach weather vocabulary to low level students.

**Acknowledgement:** We learnt this technique from Tessa Woodward.

# Party People

| Teacher | zero knowledge of students' MT |
|---|---|
| Class | monolingual |
| Level | lower intermediate to advanced |
| Purpose | to practise small talk |

**1** Put students into groups of about five. Explain that one person in each group should pretend to be a famous person from their country, but shouldn't reveal that person's identity.

**2** Tell the rest of the group to ask questions in MT to find out who the person is.

**3** When the group has discovered the person's identity, they then summarise the information they know about that person in English.

**4** Regroup the students. Arrange it so that there is at least one student from each original group in the new groups. Starting with the smallest group, give each person in the group a number, for example, one to four. Then group the class into groups of number ones, twos, threes and fours.

**5** Tell the groups that they are at a party. If you have space, let each group stand together. They should each become the famous person from their original group, and chat to the others in that role in English. You might like to play music while this is going on.

**NOTE:** Working from factual rather than invented content frees students to focus more on the language.

74

# Telling Jokes

| | |
|---|---|
| **Teacher** | working knowledge of students' MT |
| **Class** | monolingual |
| **Level** | lower intermediate to advanced |
| **Purpose** | to encourage the narrative skills involved in monologue |
| **Materials** | dictionaries (optional) |

**1** Put students into groups of four.

**2** Get one person in each group to tell a joke in MT.

**3** Ask the groups to translate the joke into English. They can use dictionaries or ask the teacher for help.

**4** Regroup the students. Arrange the groups so that there is at least one student from each original group in the new groups. Starting with the smallest group, give each student in the group a number from one to four. Then put the students into groups of number ones, twos, threes and fours.

**5** Tell the students to take it in turns to tell the joke from their original group in English.

**6** When each student has finished telling their joke, get the group to check they have understood it by telling it in MT.

**7** Tell the students to go back to their original groups. Allocate one of the jokes (not their own) to each group.

**8** Tell each group to prepare to tell the joke to the rest of the class, each student telling a part of it.

**8** Get the originators to comment on any additions, omissions or changes that have been made.

## Variations
Start by giving different groups a joke in English to retell in MT. In this way, they'll be able to tell the joke to people at home!

A good source for jokes is the Pilgrims website: www.hltmag.co.uk

This process can also be used for storytelling.

**NOTE:** It is a good idea to work on jokes before students go abroad to give them confidence in this social skill.

# Commercials

| | |
|---|---|
| **Teacher** | zero knowledge of students' MT |
| **Class** | monolingual |
| **Level** | lower intermediate to advanced |
| **Purpose** | to transfer a familiar MT text into English |

**1** Put students into groups and ask them to think of a TV commercial that they all know and could mime.

**2** Tell them to mime it to one other group.

**3** Get each group to focus on the commercial they saw the other group mime. They should work on it so that they can act it out in English.

**4** Ask the groups to act out the commercial in English to the whole class.

**5** Ask the originators of the commercial to comment.

# The Go-between

| | |
|---|---|
| **Teacher** | zero knowledge of students' MT |
| **Class** | monolingual / multilingual (at least 3 students per language) |
| **Level** | lower intermediate to advanced |
| **Purpose** | to get students to translate spontaneously |

**1** Put students into groups of three (A, B and C). In multilingual classes, put them into monolingual groups. Explain that student A is a tourist in a country where student B is a resident and student C is an interpreter.

The tourist wants to get a good itinerary for a day's sight-seeing. The tourist only speaks English, the resident only speaks MT, the interpreter speaks both. They role play this situation via the interpreter.

**2** Tell the students to change roles and repeat.

## Variation
There could be a fourth member of the group who writes down any problems the interpreter has. These can then be worked on after the activity.

This simple interpreter technique could be applied to any roleplay.

# Mumbling Stories

| Teacher | zero knowledge of students' MT |
|---------|-------------------------------|
| Class   | monlingual / multilingual |
| Level   | lower intermediate to advanced |
| Purpose | to encourage use of MT in student preparation |
|         | to boost students' performance in English |

## Preparation

For homework, ask your students to prepare to tell a story in the next lesson. The story could be one they have read but it should be one that other students are unlikely to know. It could also be a story about something that has happened to them but that their classmates have not heard already.

Each story should be 3-5 minutes long.

Tell the students not to write anything down but to adopt the following procedure:

- Mumble the story through to themselves in English.
- Mumble the story again, but this time in MT.
- Mumble it a third time in English.

Explain how useful a mumbled rehearsal can be when preparing to tell a story orally.

**1** Ask the students to start mumbling their stories through in English to make sure they are really fluent.

**2** Tell them to start the second round of mumbling. After a few seconds, call out the name of a student who should then continue to tell their story out loud while the other students hold their stories mentally at the point where they were interrupted, ready to go on at any moment. Allow snippets of two to three sentences.

**3** Call out the name of another student who carries on telling their story out loud, from where they had left off.

**4** Get eight to ten students to tell their snippet in this way.

**5** Allow the whole class to mumble from where they left off. Allow about ninety seconds for this.

**6** Have a second round of snippets, calling on the **same** students but in a different order. This way the class will hear snippets of eight to ten students' stories in English.

**7** Ask the students to gather round the story-teller whose tale they liked the best and listen to that student's story from beginning to end.

**8** The first time you do this activity, it is worth allowing feedback time for the students to express their feelings about the mumbling exercise.

**NOTE:** There are not many EFL activities that invite the students to practise language inwardly, as a form of inner monologue, and this is a valuable one. The point of the MT mumbling during homework preparation is to fill out and enrich the language of the subsequent English mumbled telling.

**Acknowledgement:** We learnt story mumbling from Anne Pechou who works in Toulouse, France.

# 5
# Using Translation

The variety and surprise elements in these activities are likely to attract and interest those of your students who don't get much joy out of learning a language. Playing with two languages will fascinate the students with strong linguistic intelligences.

These activities will also stand you in good stead if you have to teach a translation class and want to vary your methodology.

To bring back imaginative translation exercises into language teaching redresses forty years of inbalance.

# Shadowing in Two Languages

| | |
|---|---|
| **Teacher** | working knowledge of students' MT |
| **Class** | monolingual |
| **Level** | elementary to advanced |
| **Purpose** | to familiarise students with the rhythms of the English language and contrast it with those of MT |
| **Materials** | cassette / CD player |

## Preparation

Prepare two or three paragraphs of text in MT and English – or have one prepared. You could take a text from a unit further ahead in the coursebook. Record both versions of the text using your own voice or, better still, someone else's.

**1** Play the recording. Ask the students to listen to the English and the MT versions right through twice.

**2** Ask them to listen three more times. This time explain that they should 'shadow', or repeat the words fractionally later than the speaker. They should be three or four words behind, not more.

Ask them to imitate the exact pronunciation of the speaker(s) in both languages, not just to make the sounds in their own way.

At first this mimicry may provoke giggling, but students soon become involved in the activity and realise that it requires great concentration.

**3** Allow time for the students to express their feelings about the activity.

**NOTE:** This activity is taken from interpreter training. This is not a one-off activity. It should be given in short bursts regularly as the students get better and better at it.

# When Fingers Speak

| | |
|---|---|
| **Teacher** | zero knowledge of students' MT |
| **Class** | monolingual / multilingual |
| **Level** | lower intermediate to advanced |
| **Purpose** | to help students notice the difference between gestures used in MT and those used in English |

**1** If possible, work with the class standing in a circle. Ask two students to come to the board to act as scribes.

**2** Tell the students to think of a gesture involving fingers that they use in MT.

**3** One student does their gesture. Their neighbour copies it and gives the English words that would express the meaning for them.

**4** Ask the student who did the gesture to confirm or deny the meaning (different gestures have different meaning in different languages). Ask for any other interpretations from the rest of the class.

**5** Ask one of the scribes to draw the gesture on the board and the other to write the various meanings of it that the class comes up with.

**6** Repeat the process until everyone has had a chance to show their gesture.

**7** Repeat the process again, but this time get the students to make finger gestures used in English.

**NOTE:** If your class is multilingual, there will be much more interesting stuff to be shared.

**Acknowledgement:** We learnt this activity from Professor Naima Benmansour.

# Code-switching

| | |
|---|---|
| **Teacher** | zero knowledge of students' MT |
| **Class** | monolingual / multilingual (at least 3 students per language) |
| **Level** | elementary to advanced |
| **Purpose** | to allow students to move out of the constraints of English to allow weaker students to contribute more fully |

**1** Put the students into groups of three. In multilingual classes, put them into monolingual groups.

**2** Ask which students are:

only children
first-born
middle born
last-born

**3** In their groups, ask the students to start sharing their birth-order experiences and to do this in MT.

**4** After two minutes, ask them to switch to English.

**5** Repeat the code-switching instruction three or four times, so that they are alternating between English and MT for two to three minute periods.

**6** Allow plenty of time for feedback from the group on how they felt about the arbitrary code-switching.

# Excuses in Two Languages

| | |
|---|---|
| **Teacher** | zero knowledge of the students' MT |
| **Class** | monolingual / multilingual |
| **Level** | lower intermediate to advanced |
| **Purpose** | to help students notice the contrasts between the syntax and word order of English and MT |
| **Materials** | sheets of paper |

**1** Explain to the students that there is an agency in Paris that supplies men and women with sets of excuses to offer their spouses for being late back from work. It also offers school students excuses for why they haven't done their homework. Ask them to choose whether they want to work with marital or school excuses. They need to choose as a class.

**2** Ask each student to fold and tear a sheet of paper up into twelve strips. Explain that you want each person, working on their own, to write an excuse in MT on the first slip of paper. On the second slip of paper they write a second and different excuse in English. They write a third excuse on the third slip in MT, and so on, until they have six excuses in English and six in MT. Circulate, helping with the English.

**3** In monolingual classes, tell the students to mill around the room and try to get rid of as many of their slips of paper as possible. To get rid of a slip of paper, they have to exchange it with another student who has the same excuse **but in the other language**.

In multilingual classes, ask them to work with others of the same MT. If you have one Thailander, one Dane and one Tibetan for example, ask them to work together. This will involve them in translating those sentences they have written in MT into English.

**4** Explain that the winner of the game is the person with the least slips in their own handwriting after five minutes.

## Variation

If you want to work on the past perfect, simple past, past continuous and 'was going to ...' , give the students this sentence:

The man went through the red light.

Ask them to work individually and write down twelve reasons, alternating between MT and English, to explain why he did this. The second half of the activity can be done as above.

# Bilingual Chorused Interviews

| Teacher | working knowledge of students' MT |
|---|---|
| Class | monolingual |
| Level | elementary to advanced |
| Purpose | to practise giving and asking for information |
| | to diagnose a student's strengths and weakness |

**1** List three topics that you would like to be interviewed about and get the students to do the same.

**2** Explain that they are going to chorus what the interviewer or interviewee says. Practise doing this. Say a sentence and get the students to say it as you say it. Ensure that they don't just listen to a sentence and then repeat it. They must literally say it as you are saying it, so they are listening and speaking at the same time.

Practise as a whole class with them chorusing what you say and then get them to practise in pairs.

**3** Work with one student. Choose one of their topics.

**4** Arrange the class so that one third of the class is sitting behind you and the rest are behind the student you are interviewing.

**5** Tell the two groups that they should chorus whatever is said by the person in front of them (i.e., the teacher or the student being interviewed).

**6** Ask a question in English and make a note of it.

**7** Ask the interviewee to write the question in MT for future reference.

**8** Get the interviewee to answer the question orally in English. The group behind them should chorus the answer.

**9** Take notes of the answer.

**10** Continue like this till the interview is finished.

**11** Ask the interviewee to look at the first of your questions they have written in MT and translate it orally into English. Get the students behind to chorus. This enables you to assess their competence in asking questions.

**12** Using your notes, reproduce the interviewee's original answers, rewording as necessary. Get the students behind to chorus. They should note down any new language. This step can be recorded and then used both as a listening activity and an opportunity to discuss the language.

**13** Continue like this till the interview is finished.

## Extension

**1** Ask the students to choose a topic from your list.

**2** Ask one student to ask the questions in English. Take notes of the questions.

**3** Answer briefly in English and write down the answer. Tell the students to write your answer in MT.

**4** At the end of the interview repeat and, if necessary, reword the student's original questions.

**5** Tell the students to look at their MT translations of your answers and translate them back into English.

# Chant into Chant

| | |
|---|---|
| **Teacher** | zero knowledge of students' MT |
| **Class** | monolingual / multilingual |
| **Level** | lower intermediate to advanced |
| **Purpose** | to enable students to appreciate the English version of MT texts they love |

## Preparation

For homework, ask the students to choose a short song / poem they really like in MT and translate it into English. This should not be more than twenty to thirty lines.

In the next lesson, collect in the translations and select one to work on. Edit the English version, paying special attention to rhythm. Check with the student whose translation you have modified that they are happy with your changes, especially in a multilingual class or a monolingual class where you are ignorant of this student's MT.

**1** Get the student to put the text up on the board and then teach the class to recite it in the jazz-chant way.

**2** Do the same with other students' work over the next few lessons.

**Acknowledgement:** This marvellously simple technique is one we learnt at the British Council in Istanbul from a colleague named Graham. If you want more student-involving ideas like this, see *Lessons from the Learner* (Deller S, Pilgrims-Longman, 1990).

# Pass the Buck Translation

| | |
|---|---|
| **Teacher** | full knowledge of students' MT |
| **Class** | monolingual / multilingual (see Variation below) |
| **Level** | elementary to advanced |
| **Purpose** | to learn to translate fast and to practise correcting translations |
| **Materials** | OHP / sheet of A3 paper (see Preparation below), sheets of paper |

## Preparation

Choose an MT text of about ten to twelve sentences. Write it out on a transparency or sheet of A3 paper like this:

Sentence 1 in MT
English translation of sentence 1
Sentence 2 in MT
English translation of sentence 2, etc.

Have this ready for later in the lesson.

**1** Dictate the first sentence of the text in MT. Ask the students individually to translate it into English. They should write down their translation, **not** your MT sentence. Allow a timed thirty seconds for the translation.

**2** Tell the students to pass their sheet of paper to the person on their left, who should correct the translation as best they can. They keep their neighbour's sheet.

**3** Dictate the second MT sentence. Give them thirty seconds to translate it as before. Again each student should pass their sheet to the student on their left. They should then try to correct the translations of both sentences on the sheet they now have.

**4** When the dictation is over, show your own translations. Give the students time to compare and to ask questions.

## Variation

Choose an original text in English and ask the students to translate it into MT. This way round you can do the activity with a multilingual class, providing you have two or more of each language group. If it is a multilingual class, get them to pass the texts round within each language group.

# Inner Translation

| Teacher | zero knowledge of students' MT |
|---------|-------------------------------|
| Class | monolingual / multilingual |
| Level | lower intermediate to advanced |
| Purpose | to help students to do inner voice work on English – by communicating with themselves in English, they are free from the feeling of being judged by others |

**1** Do a short relaxation exercise. For example:
- Ask the students to shut their eyes and notice their breathing.
- Ask them to shut their eyes and to measure a minute in any way they wish except by looking at a clock.

**2** Ask the students to close their eyes and bring to mind a sentence in MT that expresses something they are thinking about.

**3** Ask them to say the sentence over to themselves under their breath in as many ways as possible.

**4** Ask them to think of different people saying the sentence.

**5** Tell the students to put the MT sentence into English and say the sentence over several times in their head.

**6** Ask them to find a different English translation of the same sentence and to say this new version over several times in their head.

**7** Ask the students to find a third translation and say this over several times in their head.

**8** Ask each student to write down the three English versions of their original sentence. Allow time for them to ask you language questions.

**9** Put the students into groups of four to six. Ask them each to read out the three versions of their sentences to the group and explain which one they like best and why.

**10** Do as many 'rounds' as you have time for.

**Acknowledgement:** This activity would not have happened without Adrian Underhill's 'Inner Workbench' idea.

# Speed Translation

| Teacher | zero knowledge of the students' MT |
|---------|-----------------------------------|
| Class | monolingual / multilingual |
| Level | lower intermediate to advanced |
| Purpose | to free students from the heavy influence of the English text |
| Materials | copies of text (see Preparation below) |

## Preparation
Choose a short passage in English that is well below the normal level of textual difficulty for the group. Make copies of the text.

**1** Explain to the students that they are going to translate the text into MT as fast as they can for three measured minutes. The student to translate most English words will be the winner.

**2** Give out the text face down. Count down from ten. On zero they should turn their papers over and start translating while you time three minutes.

**3** Stop the students at the end of three minutes and give them time to clear up any silly mistakes they have made.

**4** Ask them to count the number of words they have written and report to the class.

**5** If you have a monolingual class, you can ask three to five students to read out their translations, one after the other. Then invite comments on the readings.

**6** Find out who liked speed translation and who didn't and why.

**Acknowledgement:** We have used speed writing as an exam preparation technique ever since learning it from Katie Plumb back in the 80's. This is an adaptation of the technique for translation.

# Screwy Translations

| | |
|---|---|
| **Teacher** | full knowledge of students' MT |
| **Class** | monolingual |
| **Level** | lower intermediate to advanced |
| **Purpose** | to help students enjoy the humour of literal translation |

## Preparation
Collect some words and phrases in the students' MT which, when translated literally, are strange or humorous.

**1** Dictate or write a couple of idioms in MT on the board.

**2** Ask the students to give a literal translation out loud in English.

**3** Put the students into small groups and get them to make a list of phrases in MT. They then write their literal translations followed by correct translations.

**4** Each group shares their most interesting or funniest literal translations with the class.

**5** Ask them to write their correct translations on the board.

**6** Select specific words from the translations that give the students problems and work on them. For example:

> Spanish-speaking students commonly have problems with the use of 'have' and 'be' in common expressions of physical and mental states. We **are** cold or hungry in English, but in Spanish we **have** cold and hunger.

**Acknowledgement:** We learnt this activity from Tim Hahn.

# Translating Literally

| | |
|---|---|
| **Teacher** | working knowledge of students' MT |
| **Class** | monolingual |
| **Level** | lower to upper intermediate |
| **Purpose** | to encourage awareness of the problems of literal translation |
| **Material** | sheets of paper |

**1** Ask the students to work on their own or in pairs. Tell them to write an eight-line dialogue in MT. They should make it as colloquial and real as they can.

**2** Ask them to take a fresh piece of paper and translate the dialogue as literally as possible into MT. They should, for example, keep the same word order as in the MT. A Spanish dialogue literally rendered into English, for example, could look like this:

> **Pedro:** How goes?
> **Maria:** Here pulling. And you?
> **Pedro:** I find myself well but my brother is very bad.
> **Maria:** I feel it. What has passed to him?

**3** Ask individual students and pairs to swap dialogues. Tell them to turn the literally-translated dialogues into idiomatic English.

**4** Ask the students who have swapped dialogues to get together and discuss the idiomatic versions and the translation problems.

**Acknowledgement:** Simon Marshall offered us this activity for this book and we have simply edited it. Thank you, Simon.

# Word for Word into English

| Teacher | zero knowledge of students' MT |
|---|---|
| Class | monolingual / multilingual |
| Level | lower intermediate to advanced |
| Purpose | to demonstrate how differently metaphors function in 2 languages |
| | to practise colour idioms |
| Materials | copies of list of idioms, etc., copies of gapped sentences (see Preparation below) |

## Preparation

Prepare a list of idioms / collocations / chunks of language you want your students to work on. Alternatively, use the list below. Make copies of the sentences containing the words and copies of gapped sentences.

**1** Give students a list of idioms in English. Ask them to translate them word for word into MT. At this point students don't need to understand the meanings of the idioms. For example, here is a list of English colour idioms:

| | | | |
|---|---|---|---|
| 1 | a black look | 6 | a blue movie |
| 2 | red tape | 7 | green fingers |
| 3 | to be in the red | 8 | a blue-collar worker |
| 4 | out of the blue | 9 | a white lie |
| 5 | a red herring | 10 | a white elephant |

**2** Give students the idioms in sentences, to help them understand the English meaning. For example:

> 1 I got a black look when I asked for time off.
> 2 It's such a bureaucratic organisation. Full of red tape.
> 3 I don't earn as much as I spend so I'm always in the red.
> 4 I was so surprised when I got a pay rise last month. It came completely out of the blue.
> 5 Don't take any notice. It's irrelevant – just a red herring.
> 6 In many countries there are strict laws about the distribution of blue movies.
> 7 Her garden looks wonderful. She must have green fingers.
> 8 A machine operator is known as a blue-collar worker.
> 9 Sometimes we have to tell white lies in order to be kind.
> 10 The new laboratory is absolutely useless. It turned out to be a complete white elephant.

**3** Tell the students to translate the idioms into MT, using colour words where possible.

**4** Give them the original English sentences with gaps for them to fill in the idioms. Encourage them look at their list of MT idioms while they do this.

> 1 Her garden looks wonderful. She must have _____ _____ .
>
> 2 I got a _____ _____ when I asked for time off.
>
> 3 I don't earn as much as I spend, so I'm always in _____ _____ .
>
> 3 It's such a bureaucratic organisation. Full of _____ _____ .
>
> 4 Sometimes we have to tell _____ _____ in order to be kind.
>
> 5 Don't take any notice. It's irrelevant – just a _____ _____ .
>
> 6 In many countries there are strict laws about the distribution of _____ _____ .
>
> 8 A machine operator is known as a _____ -_____ worker.
>
> 9 The new laboratory is absolutely useless. It turned out to be a complete _____ _____ .
>
> 10 I was so surprised when I got a pay rise last month. It came completely out of _____ _____ .

**NOTE:** This process can be used for all kinds of metaphorical language, chunks, collocations, etc.

# Semantic Flip Flop

| | |
|---|---|
| **Teacher** | zero knowledge of students' MT |
| **Class** | monolingual / multilingual |
| **Level** | upper intermediate to advanced |
| **Purpose** | to work on contrastive syntax and grammar by translating ambiguity to help students realise that different solutions can be equally correct |
| **Materials** | copies of sentences (see list) |

**1** Explain to the students that they are going to do a 'translation-dictation' in which they write down the sentences you give them in their MT. They should write nothing in English.

Say nothing to the students about the fact that the utterances you are going to dictate are ambiguous. They will find this out for themselves.

In sentences where you might clarify the ambiguity with your stress or intonation, be sure not to do this, reading with as neutral intonation as possible.

**2** Dictate the sentences opposite.

**3** If your class is monolingual, put the students into groups of four to compare the translations they have made. If it is multilingual, put the students into monolingual groups of up to four. Any MT isolates to form an international group.

**4** Give everyone copies of the sentences in English. Ask them to compare the way they understood the English.

**5** Ask the whole class whether they found any sentences that did not have at least two translations. Go through these sentences first, drawing as much as possible from students who **did** hear the ambiguity in them.

## Variation

Forget about translation. Tell the students to write down the first sentence in English. Ask them to then add two more sentences of their own to this dictated sentence. The new sentences can be before or after the dictated one, or one before and one after, and they should add up to a coherent paragraph. Now dictate the second ambiguous sentence and follow same procedure. Use between four and six ambiguous sentences to do this.

## Ambiguous Sentences

1 We can solve your problems with information technology.
(We can solve the problems IT poses. **or** We can use IT to solve your problems.)

2 I don't like you because I work with you.
(I work with you, so I don't like you. **or** I don't like you just because I work with you.)

3 Is the dog tiring?
(Is 'tiring' transitive or intransitive?)

4 Headline: CHILD TEACHING EXPERT TO SPEAK
(Is 'child' the subject or part of an adjective?)

5 People in Devon take life slowly.
(Does 'take life' mean 'kill' or 'relax'?)

6 There are 90 odd volunteers per branch.
(Does 'odd' mean 'roughly' or 'bizarre'?)

7 I had a row with David over Christmas.
(Does this mean 'at Christmas' or 'about Christmas'?)

8 She was relieved by his appearance this morning.
(Does 'appearance' mean 'arrival' or 'how he looked'?)

9 They created a group of practically trained teachers
(Does 'practically' mean 'almost' or does it contrast with 'theoretically'?)

10 I don't like a lot of people.
(There are a lot of people I don't like. **or** I don't like too many people at once.)

11 Give me his name and I'll tick him off.
(Does this refer to a list or a reprimand?)

12 Headline: BABIES USED TO SNEAK DRUGS INTO PRISON
(How would you pronounce the 's' in 'used'?)

13 She fed her dog biscuits.
(Who got the biscuits? A woman or a dog?)

14 Along came a young mother with a small boy who was pushing a pram.
(Who was pushing the pram?)

15 The steward called the passengers' names as they arrived.
(Was the steward rude or just doing his job?)

16 Please could you walk this way?
(Does 'way' mean 'direction' or 'manner'?)

**NOTE:** You will find several more sets of ambiguous sentences on page 46 of *Dictation* (Davis, Cambridge, 1989) and on page 122 of *More Grammar Games* (Davis Cambridge, 1995).

# Delayed Translation

| Teacher | zero knowledge of students' MT |
|---|---|
| Class | monolingual / multilingual |
| Level | lower intermediate to advanced |
| Purpose | to help the student absorb a piece of English text |
| Materials | copies of text (see Preparation below), sheets of paper |

## Preparation
Chose a short, well-written text in English and make copies.

**1** Ask the students to work on their own or in pairs (their choice) and give out copies of the text.

**2** Ask them to translate it into their MT.

**3** Take in both the original and the translations at the end of the class.

**4** Some days later, give them back their MT texts and ask them to use their translations to recover the original English text as accurately as they can.

**5** Give them back the original text so they can compare it to their reconstruction.

**NOTE:** This is a powerful way of introducing students to the style of a writer whose book/s they are going to study.

**Acknowledgement:** This technique dates back at least to Roger Ascham (1515-1568) and we learnt it from Michael Benson, of Hiroshima Shudo University, Japan, who published it in *Humanising Language Teaching*, www.hltmag.co.uk, in 1999.

# Read Silently in English and Aloud in Mother Tongue

| Teacher | zero knowledge of the students' MT |
|---|---|
| Class | monolingual / multilingual |
| Level | upper intermediate to advanced |
| Purpose | to give the students the chance to enjoy the challenge of reading in English and telling in MT |

## Preparation
For homework, ask all the students to choose a children's story they like and to bring it to the next lesson. In a monolingual class, they can bring childrens' books in. In a multilingual class, ask them to each write a typical children's story in their MT.

Ask them to practise reading from the MT text straight into English. Suggest they do this to themselves 'sotto voce', mumbling.

**1** Ask the students to work individually and to mumble the texts to themselves in English.

**2** Ask them to do this again, but this time to imagine they are reading the text to a child of the appropriate age.

**3** Put the students into groups of three and ask them to read their stories to each other in English, from the MT texts in front of them.

**4** Bring the groups together and ask them how they found the activity.

## Variation
(For monolingual classes only.) Get the students to do the same activity but all working with the same MT text that they read in English. In this variation they listen to each other more critically.

**NOTE:** The more times the students do this activity, the better they get at it. This is not a one-off activity.

**Acknowledgement:** Mario learnt this technique when his mother read him Arsène Lupin detective stories in English direct from the original French text at a fast pace.

# Look, No Text!

| | |
|---|---|
| **Teacher** | zero knowledge of students' MT (see Note below) |
| **Class** | monolingual / multilingual |
| **Level** | lower intermediate to advanced |
| **Purpose** | to help the students achieve the necessary distance from the original text |
| **Materials** | copies of text (see Preparation below), coloured pens and pencils, cassette recorder, sheets of paper |

## Preparation

Choose a text in English about half a page long which will interest your students. Make copies of the text and get it recorded by three different voices. Put copies of the text up outside the classroom on a wall.

**1** Put the students into groups of three (A – C). Explain the following:

- Student A can only operate **outside** the classroom.
- Student B can only move **inside** the classroom.
- Student C must stay seated with pen and paper at the ready.
- Student A in each group reads a phrase or sentence from the text outside in the passage, meets student B at the classroom door and tells them the words.
- Student B runs over and dictates this to student C.

**2** Half-way through the activity, stop the students and ask them to all swap roles within their groups.

**3** Give each group a copy of the text and ask them to check their dictation.

**4** Play the three versions of the recorded text and ask the students to choose which voice is best for this passage. Get various students to give their reasons.

**5** Combine the groups so that you have groups of six. Ask each student to copy the whole text out, choosing the colour pen they want.

**6** Tell the students to read all the copies within their group and decide which handwriting and which colour most suits the text, giving their reasons.

**7** Collect in all the copies of the English text.

**8** Tell the students to recall the English text as accurately as possible and translate it into their MT.

**9** In a monolingual class, regroup the students in threes to compare their translations. In a multilingual class, group the students in monolingual groups and have any isolates together.

**10** Give the students back the copies of the English text.

**11** Ask them how they felt about translating a text that they did not have in front of them.

**NOTE:** In a monolingual class, if you know the students' MT, you can offer technical help at the translation stage. If you do not know the students' MT, you will **not be able** to help / interfere as the students grapple with the translation. For us it is a moot point which situation is better.

**Acknowledgement:** Ignacio M Palacios gets his students to read the source passage ten times, silently and then out loud. He takes the passage away and they translate from memory. In this activity we simply propose an enrichment of the ten readings, inspired by technical thinking drawn from Neuro-Linguistic Programming.

The **three** person running-dictation is a development of the **two** person version you will find in Davis' *Dictation* (Cambridge, 1989).

# Putting an English Advert into Mother Tongue

| | |
|---|---|
| **Teacher** | full knowledge of students' MT |
| **Class** | monolingual / multilingual |
| **Level** | upper intermediate to advanced |
| **Purpose** | to produce a text in MT that has the same pragmatic thrust as the English text though the ideas and words may be different to enhance cross-cultural awareness |
| **Materials** | copies of an advert (see Preparation below) |

## Preparation

Make copies of the advert opposite or an advert of your choice.

**1** Ask your students to read the advertisement through and ask them what the writer's intention is in the crossed out bit.

**2** Put the students into pairs or groups of three and ask them to produce a text that would have the same effect on a reader in their country. Explain that they will have to create a new text of their own in MT.

**3** In a multilingual class, ask four or five people to read out from their MT text, translating it into English.

**4** Round off with a discussion as to which text achieves the nearest to the same effect as the original.

~~You've come back from work and you are completely bushed. The kids need your attention so you bundle them into the car and drive down to the supermarket. You go round the car park twice and finally find a place miles from the entrance. Great start!~~

~~You eventually find a trolley you can sit the twins in ... sugar! You've forgotten your shopping list ...~~

~~You go up and down the aisles trying to remember the stuff you wanted to get.~~

~~'No, you can't have two Mars bars each!'~~

~~You join the queue at the check-out. Three huge trolleyloads ahead. Takes you half an hour to get to the till.~~

~~'Stop it you two!'~~

~~You load your trolley and hand the girl your card. 'This card's expired, Madam.'~~

~~You left the new one on the hall table.~~

~~You go back to the car empty-handed and the twins are now screaming their heads off.~~

~~That was a pretty rich shopping experience!~~

Why not try the **E-shopping** experience we offer you? You can send us your shopping list at the click of a mouse – any time of day or night.

We guarantee delivery within the 24 hour period.

Forget travelling at inconvenient times, finding no parking spaces, forgetting you credit card or coping with fractious twins.

**E-shopping** *is the natural way to shop from home.*

# Students Choose Songs / Poems to Translate

| Teacher | full knowledge of students' MT |
|---|---|
| Class | monolingual / multilingual |
| Level | lower intermediate to advanced |
| Purpose | to use students' own selection of texts to provide variety |
| | to motivate students by allowing them choice |

## Preparation
For homework, ask the students to choose a short poem or song lyric in their MT and translate it into English.

**1** Ask the students to underline two or three bits of the poem that they feel they have been able to translate well into English.

**2** Ask them to put their texts and translations up on the classroom walls.

**3** Give everyone a chance to read each other's translations. Go round and help with the English. If you have zero knowledge of the students' MT, you can rely on the MT speakers to make decisions about the original texts.

**4** In a monolingual class, ask half a dozen students to put up the pieces they feel they have translated well on the board together with the MT original.

**Acknowledgement:** Luke Prodromou proposed this technique In ENGLISH TEACHING *professional* in October 2000.

# From Paraphrase to Translation

| Teacher | full knowledge of student's MT |
|---|---|
| Class | monolingual |
| Level | upper intermediate to advanced |
| Purpose | to help students escape the influence of MT enough to use English fluently |
| Materials | copies of text (see Preparation below), sheets of paper |

## Preparation
This is an activity to do over two lessons. Select an English text for the students to translate for homework at the end of Lesson 1. Make copies for each student.

## Lesson 1
**1** Write these two texts on the board:
> Turning to your and D's domestic arrangements, this is what I have to say and I have been saying it for yonks, though neither of you seem to have taken it on board.

> As far as your and D's domestic arrangements are concerned, I have this to say, and have been saying it for many years without either of you appearing to hear.

**2** Ask the students to produce an MT version from the two texts.

**3** Get three students to put up their translations on the board. Lead the class through a comparison of the five texts, two English language and three MT.

**4** Give out an English text you have decided they should translate, and ask them, for homework, to write a paraphrase of it, in English, playing with both syntax and vocabulary.

## Lesson 2
**5** Put the students into pairs and get them to compare their paraphrases of the text you gave them for homework.

**6** Ask them to translate the original passage from English into MT. Circulate, helping where needed.

**7** Put the translations up on the wall for everyone to read.

**8** Round off the lesson with a discussion of the mental processing involved in paraphrasing and translating.

# Author to Translator

| | |
|---|---|
| **Teacher** | full knowledge of students' MT |
| **Class** | monolingual / multilingual (at least 2 students per language) |
| **Level** | lower intermediate to advanced |
| **Purpose** | to encourage students to find the author's message in MT text<br>to encourage sensitive translation and editing |
| **Materials** | photos (see Preparation below), sheets of paper |

## Preparation

Ask the students to bring three or four photos of themselves in the past to your next lesson.

**1** Get the students to move around the room freely. Ask them to pair off. Tell the pairs to sit together.

**2** Ask each student to choose one of the pictures they have brought in and to write about half a page about it in MT.

**3** Tell the pairs to swap their texts and corresponding picture. Tell them to translate their partner's text into English. Circulate, helping only where needed (see Note below.)

**4** Tell the students to look at the translation of their own text and help their partner where they have misunderstood or mistranslated the writer's intention. Allow plenty of time for this author-translator dialogue. Conversation may also develop about the photos / pictures.

## Variation 1

At upper intermediate to advanced level, ask the students to write their original text in English. The translation is then into the MT.

## Variation 2

Put the students into groups of three (A – C). Tell each student to write their text. Get students B and C to translate student A's text together, taking their time. Ask student A to take student B's and student C's texts and try to translate them as fast as they can. (It is best for

student A to work in one part of the room, while students B and C work in another.) They then come back together and compare the three texts and the two translation processes.

## Variation 3

You could use a whole range of different stimuli to get the writing going. A simple one is to play a piece of music that the writers react to in any way they wish. For ideas in this area, see *Musical Openings*, (Cranmer and Laroy, Pilgrims-Longman, 1995). You could ask each person to write a letter to the current owner of a house they once lived in. For more writing starters of this sort, see *Letters* (Burbidge et al., Oxford, 1996).

**NOTE:** Some people in your class may want you to look over their shoulders as they first write and then translate, to help them correct mistakes. There will be others who treasure their independence and do not want your hawk eye swooping on their writing.

Why not ask people to put a piece of paper on their table that either says:

PLEASE CORRECT   or   HELP ME WHEN I ASK YOU

Leave the choice to them.

**Acknowledgement:** We learnt this simple lesson plan from John Morgan, author of *Once Upon a Time* (Cambridge, 1984).

# Preparing to Translate an Author

| Teacher | full knowledge of students' MT |
| --- | --- |
| Class | monolingual |
| Level | upper intermediate to advanced |
| Purpose | to help students live the source of the author's state of mind, mood and way with language |
| Materials | copies of author's texts (see Preparation below), sheets of paper |

## Preparation

It would be tempting to suggest authors for this activity, but the most appropriate author is one that would appeal to the interests of your class. Once you have decided on an author, select some passages and make copies of them.

**1** Hand out copies of excerpts from the author's work and ask the students to read these silently in class. Tell them that no analytical effort is needed. They should read in a relaxed way.

**2** Ask each student to write a page in English that they think the author might have written, reflecting their mood, style and use of language.

**3** Get the students to swap their texts and translate them into MT. Circulate, offering help where needed.

**4** Tell the students to give their translated texts to the authors to comment on.

**5** Leave a few minutes for feedback on the complex processes involved in this activity.

## Variation

After the first step above, ask the students to write a piece in MT **in the style of the English author**. Put them into pairs and get them to swap passages and each translate their partner's MT text into English.

**Acknowledgements:** From Alan Maley and Ignacio M Palacios we learnt the power of writing something of your own while under the influence of a writer who is better than you. From John Morgan we learnt that instant feedback from the author is manna for the translator.

# Letters or E-mails from Home

| Teacher | zero knowledge of students' MT |
| --- | --- |
| Class | monolingual (students away from their home country) / multilingual |
| Level | lower intermediate to advanced |
| Purpose | to motivate students to translate a text fully and do any necessary editorial work on their translation |

## Preparation

For homework, ask the students to come to the next class with a page or so of a letter or e-mail they are sending to people back home or that they have received from home, together with a translation of the text into English. Tell them to choose a text that they feel comfortable sharing with other members of the class.

**1** Put the students into groups of three and ask them to share the translations they have made of their texts.

**2** Ask them to form new groups and repeat the sharing of the texts.

**3** Ask if anyone would like to read the English text to the whole class, followed by the text in MT. In multilingual classes, get two or three people with different MTs to do this. Hearing these personal texts – even in an unknown MT – can be very moving.

**4** Allow some time for whole-class feedback.

**Acknowledgement:** You will find a version of this exercise in *Letters* (Burbidge et al., Oxford, 1996). The same book brings you a lot of other writing ideas.

# Picture Note-taking in Interpreting

| | |
|---|---|
| **Teacher** | full knowledge of students' MT |
| **Class** | monolingual / multilingual (at least 2 students per language) |
| **Level** | upper intermediate to advanced |
| **Purpose** | to help students learn to interpret |

**1** Put students into pairs (A and B). In multilingual classes, put them into monolingual pairs.

**2** Ask student A to prepare to speak on some aspect of their life for two to three minutes in MT.

**3** While student A speaks, student B should listen and take mainly visual notes of what student A says. Student B may also write single words and figures.

**4** When student A has finished, ask student B to use the squiggles and pictures they have made to translate what student A said into English.

**5** Ask student A to give feedback.

**6** Ask the pairs to reverse roles so that student B speaks on some aspect of their life.

## Variation 1
Tell student A to work in English and student B to interpret into MT.

## Variation 2
Put the students into groups of three. Ask one to speak on a theme and get the other two to take visual notes. They can then compare their notes before one of them interprets.

**NOTE:** This very efficient technique is borrowed from interpreter training and is brilliant because the pictures lie between the two languages and allow the interpreter to escape from the verbal strait-jacket of the source language.

# Whispering Dictation

| | |
|---|---|
| **Teacher** | full knowledge of students' MT |
| **Class** | monolingual |
| **Level** | upper intermediate to advanced |
| **Purpose** | to help students escape from the constraints of the language they are translating from |

**1** Read a short passage in MT to the students.

**2** Tell the students you are going to read the text again, speaking some of it loudly and whispering other parts. They should only write down the whispered parts, leaving gaps for the text spoken aloud.

Read them the whole passage. Speak the first sense group, whisper the second, speak the third, whisper the fourth, and so on.

**3** Put the students into pairs and ask them to translate the whole text, recovering the missing parts from memory.

**Acknowledgement:** We learnt this activity from Ignacio M Palacios, who teaches translation in Santiago de Compostela, Spain.

# Epilogue

To advocate the judicious use of mother tongue, as this book does, is to swim **with** the irresitible flow of common sense but **against** the tide of thirty years of Western, Direct Method orthodoxy. We feel we owe it to our readers to demonstrate that the tide of Direct Method orthodoxy is now fast ebbing in the US and Europe, both among university academics and among practising teachers.

What follows are two quiet, serious voices, one from academia and the other from the chalkface, advocating sensible use of mother tongue in teaching the target language.

## A  Is there Direct Method in our Madness?

*Professor Guy Cook of University of Reading's Applied Linguistics Dept writes:*

'In the early decades of the 20th century came the Direct Method: teachers should not exploit the relationship between the students' own language and the new one. Students should not:

- translate
- learn vocabulary equivalents
- use bilingual dictionaries
- be given explanations in their first language

'Then came arguments that grammar rules should not be taught at all (not even in the target language), that errors should not be corrected, and that language should not be graded or simplified. Both the language and the classroom activities should be as similar as possible to those outside.

'These notions have been extremely influential. A whole series of well-tried activities have been outlawed:

- translation (because it involves both languages)
- deductive teaching and manipulation of forms (because they involve explicit attention to rules)
- dictation, choral work, repetition and rote-learning (because they are not how language is 'really' used)
- drilling, teaching from the front and correction (because they are authoritarian)

'Direct Method, in various guises, was the dominant methodology of the 20th century. It draws on two unsubstantiated assumptions. The first is pedagogic: that students prefer it. The second is psycholinguistic: that as children learn a first language without reference to any other, a good basis for second language learning would be to reproduce this process as far as possible.

'This central dogma – that a child is the best model for all learners – has proved durable, surviving structural, behaviourist, universalist, functional and interactive approaches. This is odd because the processes and ends of first and second language learning are obviously different. Second language learners usually end up less proficient, but they learn much faster. At a conservative estimate of 10 hours a day, a five-year-old had had 18,250 hours of meaning-focused interaction but could still only speak like a five-year-old. Any adult learner in these circumstances would be expressing serious criticisms.

'The assumptions of the Direct Method have fitted in suspiciously well with the commercial and political interests of English speaking countries. Increased immigration and mobility have made mixed language classes common within those countries. The result is that in ESL courses and EFL private language schools, the Direct Method has been a necessity. More surprisingly, it also spread to places where monolingual classes remained the norm. The strange belief developed that native speakers were the best teachers, even though they may have no knowledge of their students' language-specific difficulties. Publishers were happy, because they could significantly reduce their costs and produce textbooks for any market, irrespective of language and culture.'

(These extracts are from *Is there Direct Method in our Madness?*, first published by Richmond Publishing on their website, <www.richmondpark.net> and then re-published by *EL Gazette*. We are grateful to Guy Cook and Richmond Publishing for permission to reproduce this article.)

## B Judicious Use of the Students' Mother Tongue

*Andrew Morris, at the time of writing a member of the English Language Teaching Improvement Project, Bangladesh, writes:*

'I can't see the problem with judicious use of the students' mother tongue – especially at lower levels. For example, in many activities the instructions needed to carry out the task may be more linguistically complex than the language of the task itself. Similarly, it is important to explain to students, especially those who come from traditional learning backgrounds, what lies behind the methods we are using, and this can only be done at this level through the students' own language.

'Of course this need disappears as students progress, and should be encouraged to do so. Even at beginner levels, I try to introduce simple instructions, greetings and basic conversation in English. Nevertheless, the students' language is a useful tool and to ignore it is to waste a valuable resource. Similarly, as a learner of other languages myself, I find it necessary at times just to clarify a point of vocabulary or grammar in English, again especially at beginner level. It's absurd to operate all the time in a new second language, and ignore the many rich and valuable points of comparison there may be with their own.

'Incidentally, I've taught in a number of countries and always made an effort to learn the language. I am now a trainer in Bangladesh, and also occasionally use Bangla with teachers whose own English is weak and state a preference for this in feedback after observations.'

(On November 3rd, 1999, Andrew Morris contributed the above text to a debate on the use of L1 in the L2 classroom which had then been running for about a week on *ELTCS-L Digest* on the Web:
<ELTECS-LIST1.BRITISHCOUNCIL. ORG >
We are grateful to Andrew Morris and The British Council for permission to reproduce this article.)

# Appendix

## Students Help Each Other
page 32

### Further Puzzle Stories

1 A man with a pack on his back went into a field and died.

   (His parachute failed to open.)

2 A woman sends her son to buy three loaves of bread.
   He buys two and runs home with them.
   He runs back to the shop and buys one loaf.
   He takes this home to his mother.

   (He stutters badly when he says 'th' and is ashamed of this.)

3 A cowboy goes into a bar in Texas.
   He asks for a glass of water.
   The barman pulls out his gun.
   He aims it at the cowboy.
   The cowboy says 'thank you' and leaves the shop.

   (The cowboy has hiccups.)

4 Imagine a clearing in a forest.
   The whole forest is on fire
   In the middle of the clearing is a frogman who has water dripping from him.
   He is in great pain.

   (He was scooped up from a lake by a fire-fighting plane.)

5 A man looked up round two corners.
   He saw something that made him really want to go down.

   (The man was a submarine commander. He looked through the periscope and saw an enemy warship above.)

## Teacherless Task
page 56

### Additional Texts

---

**Blindness**

Mary was blind. She had always been blind.
She lived in Town A and the eye doctor lived in Town B.
One day Mary decided to go to the eye doctor in Town B.
She took the train to town B. On the way to Town B, the train went through a tunnel.
When Mary left the eye doctor's place, she was very, very happy.
She took the train back to Town A.
On the way back to Town A, the train entered the tunnel.
Mary opened the train door and tried to jump out. A tall man stopped her.
This is your problem: Why did she want to kill herself?

**Solution:** The doctor cured her blindness, but she knew nothing about tunnels.

---

**Lying**

Karagöz was very poor and very clever.
One day he met the Sultan. The Sultan was very depressed.
'I can make you laugh,' said Karagöz. 'I am the best liar in the world.'
'You can't make me laugh,' said the Sultan, 'but if you tell me a really big lie, I'll give you 100 gold pounds.'
'All right,' said Karagöz, 'I'll tell you a really big lie!'
'Twenty years ago your father was playing cards with my father.'
'Your father lost all his money. My father lent him 100 gold pounds.'
'My father never got his money back.'
'You liar!' shouted the Sultan, 'That's a really big lie!'
This is your problem: Did the Sultan pay Karagöz and, if so, why?

**Solution:** The Sultan paid. If he thought Karagöz was a good liar, he owed him 100 pounds. If he thought it was not a lie, then he had to pay off his father's debt!

---

# professional *perspectives*

*professional perspectives* is a series of practical methodology books designed to provide teachers of English with fresh insights, innovative ideas and original classroom materials. It is published jointly by ENGLISH TEACHING *professional* and DELTA PUBLISHING.

Other titles in the series include:

### The *Resourceful* English Teacher
*by Jonathan Chandler and Mark Stone*
A complete teaching companion containing 200 classroom activities for use in a wide range of teaching situations

### Creating Conversation in Class
*by Chris Sion*
More than 100 imaginative ideas and stimulating activities designed to get students talking in class

### The MINIMAX Teacher
*by Jon Taylor*
Practical, easy-to-use activities, methodological advice and helpful suggestions that generate the maximum student output from the minimum teacher input

### Humanising your Coursebook
*by Mario Rinvolucri*
A wide range of activities designed to extend coursebook language practice by engaging students creatively and productively

For a full list and further details of titles in the *professional perspectives* series, contact the publishers at:

ENGLISH TEACHING *professional*
Tech West House
10 Warple Way
London W3 0UE

*Tel* +44 (0)20 8762 9600
*Fax* +44 (0)20 8749 6916
*E-mail* etp@etprofessional.com
*Web* www.etprofessional.com

DELTA PUBLISHING
39 Alexandra Road
Addlestone
Surrey KT15 2PQ

*Tel* +44 (0)1932 854776
*Fax* +44 (0)1932 849528
*E-mail* info@deltapublishing.co.uk
*Web* www.deltapublishing.co.uk